POWER
Of the FITNESS MIND

Charlie S. Dannelly II

Power of the Fitness Mind

Copyright © 2016 Charlie S, Dannelly II

All rights reserved. No part of this book may be reproduced, stored in a retrieval system, or transmitted in any form or by any means, electronic, mechanical, photocopying, recording, scanning, or otherwise, without the prior written permission of the publisher.

ISBN-13: 978-0692605257

Printed in the U.S.A.

First printing 2016

DEDICATION

To my wife and best friend, Doreen Spicer-Dannelly for supporting me since day one. You've encouraged me to share my experience and knowledge of over twenty years as a personal trainer and said that if I could improve or save a few lives through my work, why not inspire and save many.

CONTENTS

Preface 1

Introduction 3

Chapter 1: The True Meaning Of Fitness 10

Chapter 2: Spiritual Fitness..17

Chapter 3: Spiritual Intelligence 26

Chapter 4: Strengthen Your Belief System 48

Chapter 5: The Scientific Power Of Attraction 52

Chapter 6: Gravity And The Power Of Attraction 59

Chapter 7: The Energy Of Fitness..67

Chapter 8: Fitness Knowledge And Your Potential 74

Chapter 9: Social Fitness..80

Chapter 10: Strengthen Your Focus...88

Chapter 11: Ancient Health & Fitness: Your Right To Be Fit 94

Chapter 12: Financial Fitness..104

Chapter 13: Successful People And Their Fitness 113

Chapter 14: Positivity Is Everything 117

Chapter 15: Fitness Minded Results 124

Chapter 16: Synchronized Fitness..131

About The Author 134

Acknowledgments 135

PREFACE

This book was specially designed to help you take your personal success in fitness and turn it into success in life. You've heard the phrases "health is wealth" and "change your body, change your life," but how hasn't been made fully clear until now. This book will give you a mental perspective, a fresher look, to get greater rewards from every effort you make. How big or small your rewards are will depend on your own personal goals and dreams. Whether you're seeking to improve your health, relationships, or finances, by applying the practices put forth in this book, you will harness the Power of the Fitness Mind and finally get the results you desire in every aspect of your life.

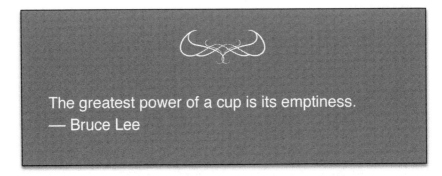

The greatest power of a cup is its emptiness.
— Bruce Lee

Before you begin each workout, start with an open mind! Do a short meditation on what you want in return for your sweat, pain, sacrifice, and hard work in the gym. Focus not only on physical results but also on mental, financial, emotional, and spiritual. Doing this will open the door for your mind and body to move in the right direction to obtain wondrous things.

INTRODUCTION

Feelings and stress are part of our connection with gravity. The earth exists because of gravity. Everything we are is because of gravity. We have evolved into the beings we are by adapting to the universal, gravitational force as defined in the laws of physics. NASA scientists, the experts on gravity, have explained how gravity effects our muscles and bone growth and even our blood regulation. We'd lose five percent of our muscle mass every week and one percent of our bones density per month if we didn't move through the forces of gravity. These same experts have also explained that gravity is not just a force but a signal that tells the body how to act. Although scientists are still exploring how this signaling transpires to make us stronger, they just know that it does. The fact is gravity exists to help us get stronger, evolve, and succeed!

So how is gravity relative to your life as a whole and to living a life of wealth? It is my belief that if we use gravity to our best advantage, we can learn to adapt and further our own personal evolution and have the life we desire. You'll see, in your own fitness mind, how gravity is important for you to get better and better at everything. The more weight you move or the more times you exercise, the stronger you get. Period. And in life, this same principle applies.

In fitness, using gravity will increase your ability in the adaptation process. In other words, when you workout there are two things that your body will use: oxygen and energy. Whether you are doing cardio, lifting weights, or any other form of exercise, you are moving through and against gravity, pushing and pulling away from that which pushes, pulls, weighs, or stresses you. It is then when you apply this movement combined with the alternate definition of gravity which is the severity or desire of something, that occupies your mind, that you can begin to use that exerted energy to become stronger, more agile, and more adaptable in all areas of your life.

Therefore, in a fitness mind that is pulling, pushing, and moving weight through gravity, whatever weighs heavily on your head, heart, and body will lead you to success.

This concept is not to be confused with the metaphysical law of attraction, which is discussed later. However, I am using gravity in its terms of physics with mass combined with its literal meaning of attraction. In the law of attraction, to put simply, you are drawing to you something in which you dwell on most profoundly. And in this law, you control what you attract. Gravity is factual and scientific, physically attracting mass to mass. However, once you've drawn that thing, that goal or desire, through the law of attraction, there will still be challenges, struggles, tests, trials, and situations, i.e. "your gravity," that you will have to work through to achieve more success and further goals.

When we have a challenge or a stressor, that is the gravity in its metaphorical sense that pulls on us constantly and to varying degrees. This is where gravity in terms of physical mass is met. This gravity will pull you to a person, place, and/or thing in which you'll use to improve yourself and your situations, and that is where the work begins. That is where you begin to chart your course to succeed. At times, we are drawn to each other because of our feelings and explore emotions. For instance, we are drawn to the gym or a health regimen because of gravity's pull on our physical body and our mental state. We all have different reasons to deal with its force, but two things are certain: gravity is constant, and it is variable in its intensity based on the weight of the mass or the situation.

Every situation in life is a weight that you have to lift. Every problem is a weight that you have to lift. Every need is a weight that you have to lift. Every goal is a weight that you have to lift. Life is a workout. Every day is a training session, and every decision is a repetition in a set in the exercise of life. And what's so great is that every effort, no matter big or small, is rewarded!

Many people, when faced with tough times, think it is a test from someone or something greater. In fitness, that "something" is the gravity in you. When you start pulling away from it instead of letting it pull on you, you get stronger and stronger until one day, you pull through and break free. The severity no longer has a hold on you, and facing that situation is a nonissue. You'll feel free as though soaring through space and time with very little effort. Then, by maintaining your strength or only making little adjustments here and there, you'll start experiencing happiness and satisfaction in your universe. This book will reveal strategies to help activate your strength in your spirit, mind, and body through fitness. My hope is that you'll never approach your workout regimen the same as you have before.

In one of my favorite movies *The Man of Steel*, when Kal-El was first learning to fly, his father told him the only way he was going to find out how strong he had become on earth was to "keep testing [his] limits." His father told him that gravity was strong, but the atmosphere was much more nourishing. Kal-El, now as Superman, tries to fly, but gravity pulls him back to earth time and time again. He fails. The symbolic thing that comes next is the very essence and message of this book. Superman contemplates his purpose, his mission, for a moment and then places his fist upon the ground and gathers his strength, and with all his might, he takes off beyond the clouds, defying gravity with ease. Although Superman is a fictional superhero, he eludes us to our own powerful capabilities.

When you feel gravity pushing on you, making things tough, don't allow it to keep you down. Instead, accept life's workout and pull away.

I always believed I had a calling for fitness. As an early teenager, I began weight lifting thanks to a Charles Atlas comic book ad. During that time, I convinced my father to buy me a set of weights. The discipline of fitness wasn't an academic course in grade school at the time, so I proceeded to find and educate myself on the subject with as much effort that was required to study and pass courses in school. My exercise routines started with the basics like jumping jacks, push-ups, sit-ups, and running. I always felt great after a workout. My results were good, but I wanted more. I went on to play football for high school then track and field in college.

Upon graduation, I immediately enlisted in the United States Military. The physical discipline I learned there still sticks with me today. However, having exited from the military, I had not decided on a career path. After confiding in my cousin Jackye, who knew my affinity for fitness, she suggested that I take a closer look at working in a health club. While driving down Interstate 10, I saw a sign. The sign said, "Family Fitness: Now Hiring." I proceeded to that location where I was told that if I was hired, I could use the gym for free. I filled out an application and was hired.

During my six years working at Family Fitness in the 1990s, I worked as a sales rep, talking thousands of people into joining the fitness revolution. I convinced them that getting in shape would be the best thing for them and their families. I was so good that I made general manager in less than a year.

As GM, I noticed that our fitness assessment and workout programs were minimal at best. Members had more questions about weight loss, strength training, exercise technique, and how to stay motivated, and the idea of a personal trainer did not even exist at the time. So I took to the idea of training some of our sales staff to receive exercise certifications to validate their interaction with the members.

I also convinced the gym owner to implement a one-on-one training session with members for a fee, so they could get the missing elements of training, giving them the attention they needed to do more than they would on their own. This one-on-one training helped to develop a relationship with that trainer for inspiration, encouragement, and accountability and gave them someone to trust in. I told my first clients that what they are doing was going to improve their health and even change their lives forever. The implementation was a huge success!

Now personal training is a multimillion dollar industry. I was on the forefront of the American fitness revolution. People were flocking in and searching for ways to become better, stronger, sexier versions of themselves. Americans were seeking to evolve. It's a time I call, "The Great Search."

Our culture was becoming more inspired to improve the quality of its existence, to become stronger, defy the effects of age, look better, own a sense of self-pride, accomplish a personal goal that no one could take from them, and strive to feel both dominant and unconquerable. Even health supplements and muscle building supplements were hitting the shelves of stores in record numbers. Companies were experimenting with all sorts of protein combinations. Bodybuilding had hit the mainstream, and the fitness magazine craze was at an all-time high. Sure, I didn't realize it at the time because I was so busy, but "The Great Search" proved to create a booming business. It seemed everyone was motivated to get fit! It was then that I started my own personal training fitness company, and after seventeen years in the business, I'm proud to say I've had success and successful clients ever since. And then one day, it suddenly hit me like a George Foreman punch.

The information that I had been accumulating over the years became overwhelming, and I saw "The Great Search" as the engine that drove this incredible fitness world that exists today, which is still evolving.

Although some people wanted to get fit, they didn't know how or where to start or how they might further benefit from their existing workout regimen. As a result, I found myself helping people get their mind fit too. The fitness mind became a frame of mind concept that I started using to help people see more reasons why they needed fitness in their life other than just physical shape, areas such as happiness, motivation, stress reduction, mental preparation for work and personal affairs, a better overall understanding of how life works around you when you're fit, and what to expect in return for your fitness accomplishments.

Since becoming a personal trainer, I've helped countless people achieve their fitness goals by applying a practice and philosophy that I had been building upon over the years. Training has exposed me to all walks of life, from Hollywood A-listers and professional athletes to Hollywood hopefuls, from industry executives to business professionals and even the average moms and dads of the world. Through this, I learned a wealth of information, including the strength of the human spirit. But I am most proud of those whom I call the Incredible 20. I've been training several of them for over fifteen years, and some have had life changing transformations. I anonymously mention some of their experiences in this book in hopes that they might be helpful to others.

Training the Incredible 20 throughout different phases in our lives has been life changing for them and for me as well. My quest to inspire my clients through fitness and health has prepared me to write this book.

I've seen firsthand that people truly want a relationship with fitness, but they are unaware of what drives them towards it or how to get started and benefit beyond their workouts. The answer they're seeking is a way to find more of themselves and discover a power that already exists inside of them.

If you keep an open mind, I believe the knowledge expounded in this book will bring you closer to who you are, where you are going, and who you can become. The immense power you possess can ultimately bring you the life you desire as a result of fitness.

CHAPTER 1

The True Meaning of Fitness

The true meaning of fitness is more than just physical exercise or achievement. It is the embodiment of the whole active self, including you and the world in which you live. This means that the physical effects of fitness will energize other aspects of your life when you not only focus on the bodily results but also the exertion of emotions.

When most people begin a journey to become fit, they are usually drawn to it for a physical desire. People want to lose weight, get in shape, build muscle, get healthy, have more energy, look better, and so on. But the question is, how and why does the desire come about in the first place? When you answer that question for yourself, this is where you'll find the secret power of fitness. Because once you get to the reason, the gravity of your situation, you will find an invitation to motivation and so much more. That is the bridge that leads you to how to "transform your body, transform your life." If you don't search that desire, you will never cross that bridge and start your journey.

The key to start is to just take one step. Notice I didn't say, "just do it." Just doing it can seem overwhelming for some people because they don't know how or where to just do it. So to get you underway, you must understand what you're up against.

Researchers have found that our personality traits, including our habits, are consistent and stable. And the older we get, the more the traits and habits become set in stone, hence the adage, "You can't teach an old dog new tricks." However, everyone is different, and as mentioned, we were made to adapt.

This brings me back to your motivation and how great your need is to get fit. Your deepest desires should be the catalyst to fight for your results. I am a firm believer that you can create change in your personality and habits. I've seen it happen with many of my clients time and time again, and I'm proud to say that they love being the new person they've become.

Now, another statistic has shown that for most people to learn a new habit the bell curve is between 18 and 254 days. So on average, it takes sixty-six days to create new habits, which become as automatic as old habits. Researchers have also found that replacing one bad habit with a good habit is the way to go.

It's also a proven fact that people who exchange cash for a service usually get results faster than those who don't. Because some habits die hard, people who have an immediate need to get fit are forced to seek assistance from dietitians, meal planners, group exercises, or personal trainers. Again, the immediacy for your desire, decision, or need to get fit is completely up to you.

Some people know what to do and how to get started, but their goal might be one dimensional. When you take the first step toward your goal, think of why you have a desire to get fit. Is it to live longer for family, for better health, or for vanity reasons? Whatever the reason is your personal preference, but let's look beyond that. How are your relationships? How are your finances? Are you handling life levelheaded, or are you running away from all of the above?

As a personal trainer, I've realized that when a person comes to me, they usually have a reason or a complaint or just need help getting better results in regards to fitness. They also bring something that has been weighing on their mind or something they were experiencing in their life that's pulling them down and draining their energy. And that is usually the gift to me and to them because now we have the key that starts the engine.

Even though we would take one step at a time at the gym, I would encourage them to train not only to focus on strengthening their physical body but also to focus on training their mind as well. As they began to adapt to the workouts and realize their own power and strength, their whole demeanor and approach began to change. Again, at first some were reluctant to adhere to the practice since they were mostly looking for physical results, but when they began to have better results in their lives, they were fully in!

In fitness, your behavior changes as you meet even your first goal. When you make the first step, whether it's going for a walk around the block, doing a circuit of weights, or just adding something green to your daily diet, it's a win even though it's small because you made the effort and succeeded. Once you see every small step forward as a success, you begin to feel accomplished, and your motivation increases. Your desire to pull away from your "gravity" and achieve more increases your ability to go beyond your initial goal because you are getting stronger, physically and mentally. Your fears about fitness diminish, and your anxiety recedes. It is as these changes occur that your results increase. Your thought process will go away from the negative thought, "I don't think I will make it," or, "I can't do this," to the positive, "I can't wait to go workout!" and, "I can do this!"

Converting your mind's responses from negative to positive is another key. By unlocking your mind's desire and maintaining a positive mental attitude as you get stronger and strive harder, you will attract positive things into your life almost like magic. When your mind starts visualizing a more positive lifestyle, you start identifying things that you did not see previously. The better your fitness level, the more types of exercises and difficulty levels you are willing to try, and you condition yourself to exercise to your body's limits so that you can build new limits. With those new limits come better results.

When you achieve goals in the other areas of your life and break through those limits, your fitness mind continues to adapt and increase its desires for more positive results. Just as your body can now handle more fitness, so can your spirit, mind, and finances handle more positive results without fear and anxiety. Just as becoming fit will burn body fat and increase muscle, causing you to look the way you have envisioned, so too can it eliminate the excess fat in your spirit, mind, and financial life. Most people don't realize the excess that they have accumulated over the years that is slowing them down and making them unhealthy, keeping them from reaching their dreams. Eliminating the excess will build a healthier lifestyle.

Now, what you feed your body during your fitness journey will determine your results. Again, true fitness is about adapting your whole being, not just your body. As we know, eating healthy foods makes a stronger and leaner body, but it also doesn't stop there.

Your mind takes in good information as mental nutrition. If you take in bad information, you will build an unhealthy mind, and the same is true with your spirit and finances. Feed your mind bad news and spend poorly, and those areas of your life will make you feel deprivation to the point of physical heaviness on your mind and heart. Feed yourself with good news and spend wisely, and you will have wellness.

The great thing about fitness is that it is never too late to start and all you have to do is say, "Yes, I want a better life." Take one small step forward and then increase your steps as your strength builds. If you feel you need a personal trainer or a nutritionist, at least you've recognized you need assistance, and that's okay. Don't let fear stop you. Personal trainers and exercise professionals can help you get better and faster results.

The same is true with your spirit and finances. Also like fitness, the effort that you put in will determine the results that you obtain. Once you take this method and place it in each category of your life, you will see your desires take shape.

Okay, this all might sound easier said than done easier, right? Not really. When you realize part of the problem you're facing is not all your fault you will begin to educate yourself and see the pitfalls that might sabotage your progress. A person who is truly fit is aware of these traps and knows how to avoid them.

In America and other great nations, automation has created an abundance of products, goods, and services that are tremendously convenient. This has also, unfortunately, led to fertile lands for addictions. The amazing growth of fast food chains, convenience stores, and the explosion of sugar products in the nation has diluted our senses, causing the obesity epidemic. By the time you are old enough to realize your addictive behavior and lifestyle, it's harder to change course and overcome, thus leading into all kinds of other addictions, daily excess, and mindless fulfillments.

We are also addicted to spiritual junk such as nonessential beliefs, actions, attitudes, and behaviors. It is this spiritual fat that is clouding our decision-making process and thus slowing us down just as too much body fat slows us down and prevents us from physically doing the things we wish to do.

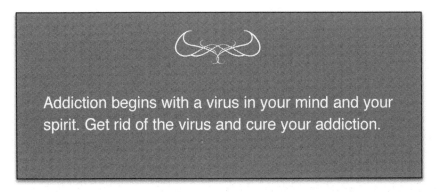

Addiction begins with a virus in your mind and your spirit. Get rid of the virus and cure your addiction.

The nation's abundance has also grown the addiction of hoarding. Not only hoarding physical things but also emotional things, like too much bad news and fear creators tugging on our emotions to the point that we need drugs to mask depression. We have a growing number of people who are addicted to being selfish, hateful, loveless, complacent, and dependent. It's unfortunate but true.

All these negative addictions add weight to your total self, making it hard for you to move through life's gravity. Your body is taking in too much, your emotions are stretched, and your thoughts are riddled with fear. The debt you have accrued in finances is at its tipping point. We have all been guilty of some addiction at some point, and these multiple addictions are filling us up and making us financially debt fat, emotionally fat, unnecessary belief fat, complacency fat, anxiety fat, dependency fat, selfishness fat, hatred fat, procrastination fat, attitude fat, and drugs fat. All these negative things in life are excess, ancillary fat. Just as in physical fitness, if you want to lose weight or reduce any of these things I have just called fat, you must work toward reducing the consumptions that are making you fat and work to become fit in every area.

"We are what we think," may be true, but I also believe there is preparation involved in achieving what we want or who we want to become. That is why fitness is so important. We must start with physical activity. Training the body creates a space in your mind to believe that anything is possible. In this modern world, it is imperative to be fit in attaining your dreams of true prosperity.

The knowledge of fitness is already written into your DNA, thanks to our ancestors, which I will explain in the chapter "Ancient Health & Fitness: Your Right to be Fit." Once you start an exercise program, you are unlocking this information that will lead you to health and wealth. By creating a system for being successful one step at a time in every other aspect of your life, there will be no limits to what you can do. Many great and successful people have used the knowledge of fitness to gain access to financial, social, spiritual, and other realms of success.

I have coined "The Fitness Mind" so everyone, in any and every society, will understand what it truly means to be fit and healthy. Whatever culture you operate under, you can use the fitness mind to become successful and to attract positive situations into your life.

CHAPTER 2

Spiritual Fitness

Spirit: The nonphysical part of a person that is the seat of emotions and character, your true self. Discovering how to shape your spirit is essential to jump-starting your fitness mind. Exercising your spirit to make it stronger will give you the energy to accomplish immeasurable things. You start with the spirit to align your nonphysical being with your physical being.

Being in fitness as long as I have, I've discovered that a lot of people are physically and spiritually separated. When some people look in the mirror, they don't see the different person they are presenting to the world. Their appearance says one thing, but their energy and true self says a different thing. It's like they're looking in the mirror that's not looking back. If people could only see themselves as they really are and accept the whole truth, the world will see them as they hoped.

Identifying your spirit means to explore your truths. Find what you believe to be true about yourself. What are your goals? What makes you happy and excited? What are your talents? What gets you up in the morning? What are your preferences sexually and monetarily? Do you desire to live comfortably, lavishly, or modestly? These are only some of the questions that might help you recognize your spirit and uncover and polish your character.

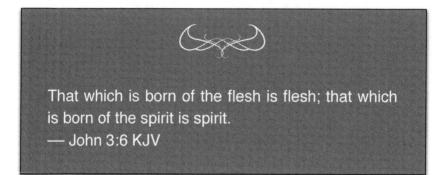

That which is born of the flesh is flesh; that which is born of the spirit is spirit.
— John 3:6 KJV

When you examine yourself and completely accept the truths about your spirit and body, you will move through life differently with confidence, and the world will respond accordingly. Allow your spirit to accept your body as it truly is whether it is tall, short, large or small. Doing this will allow your body and spirit to act as one team.

Those whose spirits act separately from their body experience turbulence in their life. They try to hide their feelings, which causes an awkward or volatile energy. Decisions are harder to make, and a full success becomes harder to achieve. A team divided cannot win. Your body and spirit are a team, and they must work cohesively. You must free yourself of some spiritual fat. Those unnecessary emotions that weigh on your character must be worked through and removed in order to become spiritually fit.

Spiritual fat or spiritual obesity is caused by filling your spirit with too many beliefs. When I first started personal training, identifying spiritual fat wasn't conceivable to me. But now I have learned over the years that if I am going to help someone achieve their fitness goals, I must identify their spiritual beliefs in order to properly address their fitness needs. Both beginners and professional fitness enthusiasts should do this. Explore and recognize what you believe and how deeply you are attached to these beliefs so that you might remove those beliefs that are weighing down your spirit. You must take inventory to get spiritually strong.

You see, we accumulate beliefs as we grow in life. Some beliefs are good, some bad, and some exist in us for no reason at all or because they were beliefs passed down through the generations. The good beliefs help our consciousness grow stronger while the bad ones are like stifling superstitions or a curse. They impede your progress for fear of something, and when you put too many beliefs in play, your state of consciousness slows down, preventing you from reinforcing a positive attitude and energy and even stopping you from increasing your self-worth. It prevents you from simplifying the truth about yourself, which is that you are a good person with a purpose who deserves to be treated with respect. You might replace this belief with another belief that you know to be true of yourself, but it should only be complimentary. No other belief should be allowed to exist in your spirit that contradicts who you truly are. It must be your prime law. You must rid your mind and spirit of any stronghold of negative beliefs. A good or right belief gives you a positive feeling in your conscious and spirit. It will permeate your character, motives, and desires and allow you to freely move forward.

This should not be confused with one's religious values, although they might be in alignment with what we should believe about ourselves. It's the external beliefs outside of one's religion that clog the spiritual arteries to our soul, contributing to a spiritual arrest, a complete collapse of our core beliefs. Outside beliefs stop us from any sort of achievement in life. Just as one goes to the gym and exercises to lose weight but then leaves the gym and eats an assortment of bad foods doesn't encourage weight loss, so too one goes to church for prayer and hope but then leaves and conducts life against those very beliefs, both consciously and subconsciously. Contradictory lifestyles impede real or substantial progress.

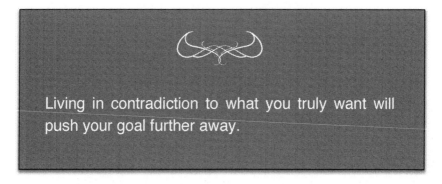

Living in contradiction to what you truly want will push your goal further away.

The ability to un-believe is not as hard as you think, but you must identify the beliefs that are causing you to act in a way that is keeping you from living your truth and attracting favorable responses. Shedding these untruths, bad beliefs, or spiritual fat can lead to achieving your deepest desires and dreams, ultimately leading to pure self-satisfaction.

I have a client, one of the Incredible 20, who was told that he could not build muscle because of a genetic defect, so he gave up trying. I had to tap into a more powerful source inside of him to give him hope that it was possible, redirect his focus, and then prove to him that what he believed in wasn't true. This belief that he couldn't build muscle kept him from achieving his goal.

We changed his spiritual diet from holding onto a long held belief of impossible success to the spiritual nutrient of the goal itself, and we were able to break through. He first removed the doubt, replaced the old belief of impossibility with possibility, and put everything toward his goal. Now, he has the strength of a professional football player, a remarkable accomplishment. His beliefs are completely in line with his continued road to even more success.

Sometimes when an untrue or negative belief has been ingrained in our mind, it becomes second nature to act on it. We even become addicted to the thought pattern that keeps us from change. Just like becoming full of addictive foods, we become addicted to emotional junk and negative comments and continually feed them to ourselves without even realizing the damage we're causing. You can even be addicted to bad behavior itself, including procrastination. All this spiritual junk becomes a way of life that's unhealthy for success. The point is that when you are full of stuff that weighs down your spirit, stomach, heart, and mind, you can't move or won't move. Getting rid of spiritual junk is just as important as removing anything else that's dangerous to your health. It plays a huge part of your progress going forward.

Another client in the Incredible 20 was going through a tough time in her marriage, ultimately leading to a divorce. During this time, she remained a client and continued her physical training. I had not realized the secrets of fitness until later, but I continued to observe her. I watched her body physically change, going from beautiful and confident to sickly and shameful. Her hair was graying fast and falling out. She was losing weight at a rapid pace. Her eyes were sinking into her skull with bags developing under her eyes. Her skin was becoming brittle and pale. She started getting skin sores for no reason. And sadly, she didn't care. She became full of doubt, embarrassment, hate, regret, confusion, disappointment, depression, loneliness, and vengefulness. These were the results of all the spiritual fats she had consumed. And although her body was thinning, she was becoming spiritually obese.

The bad information she was taking in was an attack to her character, making her spiritually fat, and her body was responding accordingly. She attempted to compress and internalize everything. This is the same as hiding the fat on the body, holding your stomach in or wearing compression undergarments. You can try to hide it, but the mass is still obvious. The discomfort still affects how you communicate with people.

Fortunately, she kept training, and as her personal trainer, I was able to observe and continue to care for her physical well-being on a consistent weekly basis. The fact that she kept her schedule made me realize that she cared about herself and believed something about training was good for her even if it was at the very least.

One day during our training session, she asked me, "What should I do with my life now?" It was at that moment that I had sight for a course of action for her to change. First, I began with changing her exercise routines. Then I convinced her to do a short meditation in front of me before each workout. I would give her positive words to focus on during her meditation, and I would mention those words and talk about them with her during her workouts, keeping her mind focused on those words. We did this over and over until one day she said, "I am going to change my whole life. Will you help me?" I had already started.

Today, she is one of Hollywood's most powerful women. People that knew her then and see her now said, "Wow! You are beautiful. What did you do?" They could barely recognize her. She has a brand new job and is thriving, traveling all over the world and developing relationships with the most powerful people on earth. And to think that this all started with one word, the first word I asked her to meditate on: *believe*. If she could believe that the *change* she desired was possible, then it would happen. She focused all her energy to improve and redesign her life, and she did. So, yes, it is possible to build a new world of your own starting with just one word.

As life happens, we consciously and subconsciously allow ourselves to become clouded or too full of meaningless and negative beliefs, creating doubt and bogging us down with spiritual fat, thus weakening our power. So, by diminishing or deleting old and irrelevant beliefs about yourself, you can strengthen your focus, increase your power, and create positive and meaningful changes or results in your life.

When you work hard, you expect to get results. This expectation is a powerful force that children use instinctively. Children have the most amazing ability to expect. They expect good things to happen when they do something good. Whether they score big on a game or a test or have a birthday, they look for something to be produced for their reward. It is that same amount of expectation we should readopt in adulthood.

As we become adults, many people let their sense of expectation go, making them feel powerless. Disappointments have stunted our sense of high expectation because we've been let down numerous times or things just didn't go as planned. However, it is now essential to reignite the power of expectation if you want positive changes in your life. Doing this will reinforce your belief that goals and desires are possible.

And what's more, when you put yourself in a position to expect something, the chemical balance of your body changes in order to keep you motivated to achieve a goal. When you achieve that goal, the chemicals in your body shift, causing the sensation of gratification. That's why taking up fitness is such a powerful tool to strengthening your beliefs, spirituality, and chemical balance.

> Truly, I say to you, unless you [change] and become like little children [trusting and forgiving], you can never enter the kingdom of Heaven.
> — Matthew 18:3 KJV

When I interview new clients and ask them what they expect from reaching their fitness goals, over 90% say they want to look like a particular image of a person in a magazine or they say they want to look the way they used to. Although this is an expectation, often times it's unrealistic. Magazine photos are altered for impact, and old pictures of people don't reflect the natural changes that have happened to their body other than weight gain. It's not my job to destroy their dreams but to get them to the best version of themselves today. And 100% of the time, they are satisfied with their results even more so than looking like the old them or some photoshopped picture. But again, without the attitude of expectation, obtaining any positive results would have been hard.

It is this spiritual fat that is clouding our decision making, thus slowing us down. Just as too much body fat slows us down and prevents us from physically doing the things we wish to do, spiritual fat also slows us down and prevents us from moving in the right direction in life.

CHAPTER 3

Spiritual Intelligence

In physical fitness, the more goals you reach, the more attuned you are to your body and able to test its strengths and limits. Your body learns about itself through exertion, exhaustion, fatigue, sweat, recovery, sleep, stress, and strength and exposes your weaknesses. As your body endures these physical events, it attempts to overcome them by making incremental adjustments as you proceed with your fitness goals. This is in part known as muscle memory. Your muscles are building upon and recording each time it's under stress. This becomes an intelligence that allows your body to adapt its physical strength and depends on it to get stronger. As with your spirit, it too has an intellect that allows or denies strength for a healthy self-worth and positive growth. To that point, physical fitness and your spiritual intelligence go hand in hand.

In other words, your body is constantly adjusting to the demand the mind has set out to achieve. When the body reaches a new level of fitness, it bookmarks that level so to speak to make it easier to reach the next time should you digress for any reason. However, there's a time limit. The longer you are away from exercising, the weaker you become. "Use it or lose it" applies.

So the question is, what does this have to do with the spirit's intelligence? Here is the connection. Most people think that the mind is in control of the body. I challenge this notion. I believe the body is in control. The brain only collects and records information to use when necessary. The body has responses to certain things that have nothing to do with memory or information. For example, physical attraction is purely spiritual and a bodily response. Other things people are drawn to for fun, excitement, or relaxation or even a career are most often followed instinctively by the spirit and not always from memory. So if the mind were in control of the body, you wouldn't have desires, something your spirit greatly needs to guide the body and mind to achieve goals.

When people decide to improve their health and fitness and seek a personal trainer, they are bringing to me a collection of information that their body has been exposed to. Their body pushed them to the point to make the decision to do something about their health, fitness, physical appearance, or overall well-being. And even though these people have become aware of their current physical condition, they must first have a desire to improve it. It is that desire to change that opens the door for the power of expectation. And as those expectations of physical improvement are obtained, choices to change or improve other aspects of your life have a greater possibility of following suit.

> We should take care not to make the intellect our god; it has, of course, powerful muscles but no personality. — Albert Einstein

Our intelligence encompasses many different learning experiences, trials, successes, and failures. Each mind has at least one strong talent or ability, such as problem solving, artistic sensibilities, being an orator and communicator, healer, teacher, and many more, that they can rely on to make the best decision for them to further their spiritual desire. However, you must have that desire to use it to your best advantage. Not using it at all will keep you from progressing.

In fitness, if you use your body's intelligence to accept the improvements in your body, you are welcoming change for your spiritual needs. You can use this type of motivation in other areas of your life as well. For instance, if you find yourself in a situation that you would like to see a change, find the courage to deal with it in a new way. Whether you succeed or fail, you're strengthening your thought process, which will eventually lead you to a solution. This will make you stronger in your thinking and reward you with positive results, not weaker with no or negative results.

Sometimes we struggle with identifying the reasons why we can't or won't progress even if our spirit has the desire to. After working for many years with people on a physical fitness level, I found myself in a confessional based relationship with many of my clients, and I've appreciated their trust. In this, I've identified five areas of the human spirit and the effects that fitness has on them. The following five areas are your emotions, fears, awareness, insight, and judgement. Learning how these play a role in strength or weakness will allow you to clearly see the road blocks on your way to success. There's immeasurable power to be gained in recognizing these issues. Let us examine your spirit so we might strengthen your spiritual intelligence.

Fitness And Your Emotions

In life, we are governed by our emotions. Whether we're experiencing the typical emotions of being happy, sad, content, discontent, angry, frustrated, or even-keeled and satisfied, our growth depends on how we handle our emotions. Our fitness success or failure will also hinge upon our coming to grips with our emotions. And since most of our emotions are experienced through relationships, we must explore those relationships to use what gravity lies there to pull us through.

Your relationships with loved ones, friends, family, coworkers, and even your relationship with your career, food, and health are all a part of what makes you an emotional human being, which exposes your faults and weaknesses. And this is where you can find the potential to get stronger in your spiritual intelligence.

But to start, there must be a certain preparedness. Just as a child entering adulthood, the body and mind are constantly preparing to take on more responsibility and challenges in life. In fitness, we must prepare our minds to garner emotional strength if we want to succeed not just in fitness but in life.

One of the Incredible 20 was a young lady who had reached the top 1% of financial status in America. When she came to me, she realized her lifestyle had change. Striving for success in her work took a toll on her body and well-being. Although she wasn't overweight, she felt out of shape.

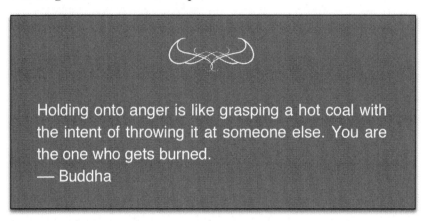

Holding onto anger is like grasping a hot coal with the intent of throwing it at someone else. You are the one who gets burned.
— Buddha

After about six months of consistent sessions, she had lost a considerable amount of weight and was in great physical shape. She finally achieved the body she wanted. Then she got into a relationship that was wonderful at first but soon turned toxic.

In the relationship, she found herself going down a dark path. Unfortunately, she allowed the man she thought she could love and trust control of her feelings. She gave him her heart, and he took advantage of it with no consequences to himself. And after all he had done, she still felt obligated to him. Through all the pain and all the misery, she still gave him chances.

When she finally tried to stand up for herself, he left her. He knew she could not handle the abandonment, but he left without a trace, never to return. This was devastating for her, but he was right. She had been dealing with abandonment issues all along.

Her level of negative emotions spiked. Things began to fall apart. Her thriving business plummeted, and she lost many of her friends. She cried daily for months and sought relief using drugs and self-abuse. All the work she had put in making herself beautiful evaporated. The tumultuous relationship broke her spirit and left her angry.

Now, it gives me great pleasure to say that I saw the rise of a champion in this very same woman. Through all the hardships she was enduring, she continued to train, which I am so grateful for. I believe I was a constant advisory at the time, but I could only hope that she would recognize the gravity of her situation, the abandonment she had endured many years prior.

How was this relationship trying to strengthen her spirit? Although she survived, it took eighteen months of rehab to restore her nerves. The gym became her new place of peace where she could focus on herself each day before facing the world. During that time, she was trying to figure out how a strong woman such as herself could have let a bad relationship tear through her life. Sometimes it takes a failing situation to make you recognize an emotional landmine, but it's how you emerge that makes all the difference. And in this case, my client is much stronger than ever, and I couldn't be more proud of her.

I believe if you look into our life before you make decisions to embark on a relationship with anyone or in anything, you should ask yourself, do you have the emotional capacity to handle success or failure in it? Are you prepared? Do you have the emotional strength to stop the relationship and recover without major damage in the event it does fail?

Going into a relationship, any kind of relationship, with all positivity is great. It's what you should do. But since you never truly know what kinds of issues might arise that could be detrimental to your health, you must be prepared to cut ties, regroup, and get back on track. The fact that most of us don't deal with ourselves before we go into a situation makes us emotionally vulnerable. We leave the door open to be disappointed, especially after failure. We mustn't do that. We must get prepared.

In fitness, it is important that you develop a plan to increase your emotional strength before you start. Just as a personal trainer will develop a plan to make your body stronger and look and feel better, so should you do the same for emotional fitness. Learn how to look inside yourself to find the times in your past that might be holding you back today. Have you allowed your emotions to get the best of you, or are you able to use that gravitational pull to benefit you by pushing through it? Mentally play back those events as an outside viewer and critique the events. This will help you handle the stress of a weakness or failure and give you the ability to handle it.

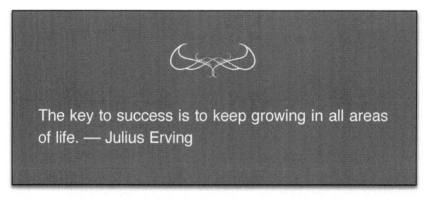

The key to success is to keep growing in all areas of life. — Julius Erving

Almost in all things, failure can make you stronger. It's about perspective, recovery, and resiliency. In fitness, failure makes you stronger after recovery. Meaning, if you pressed or pulled weight past the point of fatigue and simply couldn't do one more rep and were forced to stop, that is called "pushing to failure." It's actually healthy because the body immediately gathers energy to restore itself.

With emotional failure, you have an opportunity to get stronger as well. By learning from past events, you can prepare yourself emotionally for the future. Just as the body learns to recover faster and faster, so too should you train your emotions to recover. This will ultimately become a part of your spiritual intelligence from which you can draw strength.

Now, I don't pride myself on giving advice on personal relationships—there are plenty of advisers out there for that—but I do think it's healthy to consider your emotional feelings before going into any type of relationship. Be it with a person, a workout program, or anything in between, give yourself short-term and long-term goals. For each goal, be determined for success, but in the event there's failure, know that there's strength in that as well. This mind-set makes every situation a win-win situation. You'll be prepared for a positive outcome in any relationship.

Having a winner's edge can guarantee you positive results. For example, let's say you decide to gamble in a casino, and you budget $1,000 to play with. If you win, celebrate. You've successfully taken a risk with your money, which took time and energy to earn, and now you've made more from it. However, if you lose, you can recover because it was in your budget. You prepared ahead of time, win or lose. You are good either way. But if you disregard your plan and withdraw more money to gamble with and you lose again, it will be harder to recover from the ripple effect of negative results in your emotional well-being. Again, in any relationship, you're taking risks with your time and your energy. Being prepared allows you to take risks responsibly and be more focused on success at every level. While success by failure is not necessarily a bad thing, it might keep you from achieving your ultimate goal sooner.

When you make a deal with yourself to obtain a fitness goal, you might fall short. However, give yourself credit for what you have achieved. Take note of what you've learned about yourself and then recover, regroup, and move on. If you've tried working out on your own and failed, you've learned something about yourself and your process. Maybe reevaluate your approach and try again. Do not allow the gravity of that failure pull you down so much that you give up. That is an opportunity to explore your emotions and strengthen yourself through what pulls on you. Getting back up is where you find that inner champion.

> Keeping the body in good health is a duty. Otherwise, we shall not be able to keep our mind strong and clear. — Buddha

Do whatever it takes to start again. Maybe the first step is not showing up at the gym or downloading a workout plan. Maybe it's going to your place of worship or a place of peace or confiding in a friend that might help you emotionally prepare to move in a progressive direction. Read self-help books on how to free yourself of emotional issues and so on. This will prepare you for what's to come when success hits because it starts as soon as you take that first step. As I've mentioned before, every effort is rewarded. If the desire is there, so will your body and mind follow.

Fitness And Your Fears

As a personal trainer, I am used to first-time clients showing fear or developing anxiety before a physical exercise session. I see it as a natural response that occurs due to exposure of the unknown. They seem riddled with fearful thoughts. They don't know what to expect, if they're going to be able to go through with their first session, or they'll be embarrassed by their exposed weakness. I've also found that when fear sets in, there are no words that can rid you of it. The only thing that puts their fears at ease is the actual completion of the experience. Once they begin listening to my instructions and commands, they get lost in their tasks. When they're done, the fear has dissipated and replaced by relief, and that's what physical fitness can do with most of your emotions. The body requires this relief for balance and well-being.

Although we experience many emotions, the one emotion that weighs us down the most is fear. Besides our normal, everyday fears having to do with family, loved ones, and ourselves, there are outside alarms that attempt to frazzle our nerves regularly. The media is constantly breaking news on an outbreak, the wars, and other world-ending reports that keep our fear on high. Sometimes, it's hard not to be overrun with fear, but we must not let that happen. Overcoming fear is one of the most important steps you'll take if you want to experience change, progress, and success.

The dangerous aspect of fear is that it has the power to immobilize you from moving forward even one step. How many times have you talked yourself out of something that could have been a good thing, like trying something new in regards to fitness? You doubted, you rationalized, and before you knew it, you dropped the good idea all together. What happened? You allowed fear to creep in, and you gave it power by allowing it to feed off your imagination instead of allowing inspiration to feed. Do yourself the greatest favor and allow optimism to keep fear out. Allow your desires to drive you towards what good will come when you take the first step. When you do, exercise will repay you abundantly, including other emotional relief.

Succeeding at a short-term task feeds the brain's reward system, which in turn fuels your confidence, thus lowering your level of fear. It is impossible to eliminate fear altogether, but you can learn to use its presence as fuel to do something positive in your life. Begin with planning a short-term goal. Pick something that you really want and yet causes a great amount of fear, something that you have talked yourself out of before, but this time stay optimistic. You won't be disappointed.

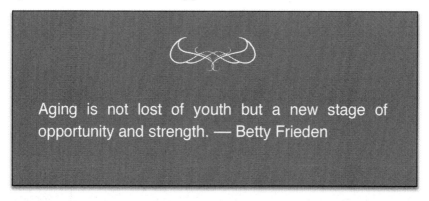

Aging is not lost of youth but a new stage of opportunity and strength. — Betty Frieden

By taxing the body physically with different fitness tasks, the brain begins to benefit almost instantly. A shot of endorphins, the feel-good hormone, and the feeling of achievement are two reactions that cause the brain and the body to reset together. Doing this repeatedly gives a person a tremendous health and quality of life advantage over ordinary life. The brain functions faster; the body works better. Memory and memory recall work better. Your level of emotional fear is rebooted practically to zero, and when fear is low, decisions can be made without hesitation and with confidence.

You might have heard people who have conquered their fears say they feel invincible, fearless, or that they feel like they can conquer anything. Going forward, they didn't allow fear to set in because optimism and confidence now occupy that space. They've rebooted their emotional system. But since fear, like all emotions, attempts to enter your spirit at any time, you can see why consistent daily or weekly sessions of physical fitness are needed.

As a personal trainer, one of my personal quotes is "Hate me now; love me later." New clients tend to hate me constantly telling them they can do something physically when their minds are set on fear and disbelief. But once someone achieves what seems unachievable, something magical happens. Suddenly, they want more. And when they are faced with another seemingly impossible physical task, they are willing and eager to try even if they fail the first time. They are telling themselves that they can do it the next time. I have found that this boost in confidence would not have happened if it weren't for that first task. As I mentioned, make sure your spirit and your body are looking at each other and know each other. In other words, make sure your inner self and your physical body are in agreement.

One of the Incredible 20 is a beautiful lady in her early forties. She is in perfect shape and looks fifteen years younger than her age. A younger, very handsome Swedish man spotted her in a restaurant and introduced himself. Before she had a chance to take a deep breath, the two of them were dating. She was having the time of her life, yet she feared that once he knew her age, he would run like a frightened rabbit. She asked me what she should do. I said tell him. I told her he liked her for who she was, not how old she was. She resisted.

Then, one night after a lovely meal and a romantic stroll on the beach, he told her that he loved her. She was shocked. And although she felt the same, she was too fearful to tell him because of her age. She admitted to me her fear, and I told her, "Fear is fear. It may look different and feel different, but it is the same fear, just like sugar. Sugar is the same no matter where it is. And just like you can choose not to use sugar, you can choose not to use fear. In the gym, you overcome those impossible tasks by focusing on using your strength, and you are able to use your strength because you know it is for a finite amount of time. Do the same with telling him what you truly want. Tell him your deepest desires and why he is a part of your deepest desires. If he is attracted to your deepest desires, then he has the motivation to make you happy. Regardless of age, what you truly want deep down inside of you is what attracts in a relationship. If your deep desires aren't experienced, then at some point in the relationship, you will face unhappiness. Just as in the journey of fitness when you set out to get in shape, you had a vision of what you wanted your body to achieve, so too is your spirit with regard to your deepest desires."

One night, she chose not to allow fear to interfere and told him her age and proceeded to tell him her deepest desires, that she loved him and that she felt as if the two of them together could conquer the world. She told him if he asked her to marry him she would say yes. That next year they were married and, because she was in such good shape, the two of them had kids. She still goes to the gym and uses the principles of fitness to help see and guide her life.

As with fitness, so too can you strengthen your emotions to conquer fear one step or goal at a time. No one said that losing the weight of fear would be easy. Just as losing weight takes effort, so too does losing fear. And just like body fat, if you don't constantly stay aware of your fears, they will accumulate to the point of spiritual paralysis, a state where you have no control over your emotions. Avoid spiritually digesting new fear. Work on eliminating old and accumulated fear and focus on working toward feeling relief from that fear. Update and reboot your fitness mind by going on a spiritual diet and exercising your spiritual optimism.

Fitness And Your Awareness

By definition, awareness is the state or ability to identify subjects, objects, and general surroundings or to recognize events and sense patterns. Sense data, what we've learned by being aware, can be confirmed by an observer without necessarily implying understanding. In biological psychology, awareness is defined as a human's or an animal's perception and cognitive reaction to a condition or event. When you put the meanings together to explore this level of consciousness, it means simply that although we know what surrounds us, where we are, and what we're doing, we don't always take the time to understand why we are where we are. In this, I'd like to add that sometimes we aren't even aware of who we really are and what we're capable of moment to moment. I've seen clients time and time again go through a metamorphosis once they become fully aware of their whole self, mind, body, and spirit. Strengthening your spiritual awareness will help you understand just how powerful you are.

In the process of becoming physically fit, your mind becomes exposed to your body's current physical capabilities and how to improve them. It also gives you a closer view of how your body is operating on the inside. You start to pay attention to your body through the following sense data: observation, education, and self-admiration. Learning more about your body's health and condition and physically monitoring your body by measuring your weight, waist, hips, et al., will become new habits. Each individual pays attention to his or her body differently, but usually the attention grows as your fitness results increase. But again, it's not just about physical changes and having a more positive attitude, it's about challenges that arise that give you an opportunity to take a closer look inside. That is key to developing a more sensitive state of self-awareness.

The greater part of human pain is unnecessary. It is self-created so long as the unobserved mind ruins your life. — Eckhart Tolle

One of the Incredible 20 was a middle aged lady who had spent several years in the entertainment industry. As the industry became more and more technical and less theatrical, she perceived herself as being outdated. After numerous attempts at learning technical skills, she became distraught. She began losing self-esteem and self-worth. She felt as though she did not belong anymore. She gained weight and lost her desire to look presentable, mentally falling into the abyss of feeling rejected. She was recommended to me, and she only acted on the recommendation as a last resort.

When the training started, I found that she was athletic and had a strong heart. I asked her if she played any type of sports early in life. She said she ran track, but you would not have known because of her current weight. I used that information and mimicked what her body used to do in track practice but in small increments. I kept her focused on each achievement as she began to regain her strength. Soon, she began to recall past successes in her career and earlier life. Hearing her talk proudly of herself showed me that she was regaining her self-esteem. Low and behold, losing the weight came quickly, and her achievements gave her a sense of encouragement.

I realized that she had become unaware of her athletic ability, but more importantly, she forgot what triumphs she had, how strong she was, and that her muscles' memory was still intact. By getting her to focus on her physical body and exert energy, she was able to become fully aware of her capabilities and tap into the success she once was and still is.

I asked her what she was trained in when she first started in the entertainment industry. She said, "I started as a writer," and she proceeded to tell me that she had run the gamut in the industry becoming a producer, director, and even a creator. I quickly realized that her current career status had kept her from going back to the basics. It was fear and bad beliefs. Because of that fear, she had become unaware of her true value. So I asked her what technical job closely relied on a writer's skill other than the jobs she had. She replied, "Editing."

After numerous free sessions, she had a much better outlook. So I asked her if she would entertain a suggestion from me. She was open. I asked her to contact a known editor and volunteer her time twice a week to help them streamline their editing using just her writer's eye. She would sit with the editor and assist by helping with attention to detail on the script. She agreed, and the editor liked her work so much that he recommended her to a major studio for work as an assistant editor. After losing close to sixty pounds and gaining a new skill set and new sense of self-awareness, she was ready for more. She later took a meeting with the studio for a job as an assistant editor and ended up with a writing deal for a television show.

Unlike previous client scenarios, this experience taught me that when a person improves their body, their desires almost automatically increase. On the surface, it's the classic "look good, feel good" experience, but it's more than that. When you use fitness coupled with your gravity, your outlook improves, and your confidence and your courage increases exponentially. It will cause you to pay more attention to your needs and habits, and it will directly affect your personality and how you value yourself. This new self-awareness will cause you to seek opportunities that were previously ignored or forgotten. Companionships, leadership positions, and financial increases will all feel within reach. Positive results in all different aspects of your life will seem possible. Strengthening your self-awareness will move you to self-actualization and draw you closer to success in many aspects of your life, causing a more powerful spirit.

Fitness And Your Insight

Spiritually, we are known to use some level of insight, meaning we have the ability to understand ourselves, people, and situations in a very clear way. By focusing more deeply within ourselves, we will find that we have an innate ability to comprehend our own motivations and behaviors because of our insight. It is at the very core of our spiritual intelligence. If we tap into it, we can use it to our best advantage for continual success and greatness in fitness.

If you've known an intuitive or someone who has the gift for "seeing" into the future, he or she will try to predict the future or have a view of what's to come. Most of us possess this very power, but many of us ignore it or don't give it much attention. Using your own insight can help you find comfort and strength. When you search under all the layers of your fears, your learned beliefs, and even your awareness, you'll see what you've known about yourself and your abilities since the moment you were conscious of your inner voice. The seat of your soul, your spirit, has its own oracle that guides everything you do. It will help you if you would only listen.

In fitness, I've seen people have goals, reach their goals, then stop at that level, plateau, or let everything fall apart and fall back under the layers of fear and bad beliefs and no longer be aware of their greatness.

Have you ever gone on a diet but then the minute you reached your goal, you went back to old habits and gained the weight back? Here's the problem: You were not meant to just diet or even diet and exercise temporarily or even call the way you eat "a diet." If you look toward your insight, you know what's good for you and what's not to achieve what you foresee of yourself in the future. You know the problems because your body has begun to complain in the form of excess weight, stress, malfunctions, and emotional duress. Whether you've educated yourself or not on what's best for you, your spirit knows how to prompt you to take a closer look and even educate yourself if you haven't done so. It will tell you not to diet in the fade sense of the word but find what works best for your total body, including exercise and what foods to eat.

Insight also plays an important role for not only obtaining success but enjoying it. Having insight confirms your true belief about yourself and your ultimate goal in life. Once you've researched your spirit know what your goal is, you can proceed to move forward with awareness of that fact. In fitness, you must have a goal in mind and *know* that you can achieve it because it agrees with your ultimate goal. As mentioned earlier, you must *believe* achieving your fitness goals are possible, but you must also maintain balance in order to keep the level of success you've accomplished. It is one thing to achieve success and another to have the insight to enjoy it in the healthiest way possible.

The more successful you become, the stronger your insight should be. For instance, a business owner knows when it's time to expand or make additions to his or her company. Demands become evident, consumers are faithful and asking for more, the work staff is operating at optimal ability, and performance and profits are exceptional. Growth is beckoning. The same analogy applies in fitness. As you accomplish your first goal, you'll become stronger, lose weight and/or inches, achieve a new sense of self, you'll press on to higher heights or switch up the routine to maintain that accomplished feeling. When you reach a plateau in fitness, add more intensity to your exercises or choose different ones to continue acquiring success. Your insight can give you the ability to see your current status as progress so that you can make other moves to keep you on course to higher goals.

In business, life, and physical fitness, it takes continued insight to foresee your challenges and plateaus. Losing your insight as you grow in success can become a problem and cause you to plateau and keep you from progressing. That's why it is important to stay in physical shape, get the standard amount of sleep, improve your diet, and be aware of your overall health. Let nothing come before your health. Without it all, your goals are limited or even diminished.

The added bonus to maintaining a consistent schedule and range of exercises is that the serotonin levels in your brain, which helps clear your mind and helps you make good decisions, will stay elevated. It will keep you sharp and focused on your ultimate goals.

Fitness And Your Judgment

During the process of becoming physically fit, a new outlook begins to happen, and you will acquire a higher understanding of life itself. This will cause you to use better judgment for yourself in all things. When you act on the desire to get fit, you've made a good decision, and it only gets better. As you continue a life in fitness, using better judgment will become like second nature.

You may not notice at first, but one of the great things that happens when you begin a workout regime is the rest of your daily life will become organized and synced to support the good changes that are occurring. The commitment, the routine, the meal planning, and the monitoring of results are all part of the program that will compel you to continue using better judgment in other areas. It's as if you've activated a new area in your spirit to do things differently than you have done before. As you feel brighter, quicker, and smarter, it's not something you'll want to stop, especially because you'll begin to see how this new personality shift is changing your evident energy. And if you correlate fitness with life, you will see how you can have significant advantages in business, social communication, physical attraction, and competitive situations.

>
>
> We should not pretend to understand the world only by the intellect. The judgement of the intellect is only part of the truth.
> Carl Jung

Just as your body becomes stronger, your judgments become sharper and more accurate, functioning at a higher state and giving you remarkable opinions and extraordinarily accurate decision making. Those that have discovered this know the feeling and rely on it. This happens because the body's state of being is at an optimal peak in energy, functionality, clarity, consciousness, and confidence. It is in this form of clear judgment that creates breakthroughs in life.

Using the state of fitness to strengthen your overall spiritual well-being lifts your presence among people. A person who trains for a marathon and prepares more than any other, their performance will lift them above their competitors, ultimately becoming a champion. In the same way, this new spiritual strength will propel you ahead of the pack. When other spirits are down, yours will endure. It is this spiritual endurance that will, in tough moments, help you to maintain great clarity. And those who see your spiritual strength will push favorably forward, keeping in mind that your heightened spiritual mind sees the world from another perspective.

Through fitness, a higher sense of well-being permeates throughout your body and mind. This is no ordinary occurrence, but to reap these benefits, you must put yourself in a complete state of a fitness mind—physically, spiritually, emotionally, and mentally.

CHAPTER 4

Strengthen Your Belief System

How strong is your belief system? Your spiritual strength will depend on what you believe to be true about yourself. The activities that you do, things you say about yourself, and your behavior on a consistent basis will have a direct effect on your belief system. Exercise can give your belief system a boost in that it requires positive responses, emotions, and results. It causes you to reinforce your attributes and recover from any setback or failure.

When you strengthen your belief system through fitness, you automatically transfer a portion of that belief into other elements of your life. The more results you obtain through fitness, the more you believe in yourself with other things in life. When you obtain a fitness goal, you experience the sensation of discovering belief. I say *discover* because when you achieve something, you believe it. You saw with your own eyes that you are capable. When a scientist discovers something, he is elated because he has the facts to believe it. The power of belief is a fantastic physical stimulator. Choose to believe in facts first. List the things you believe in, the things that move your life, the things that cause you to make decisions, and see if those beliefs are allowing you to move in the positive direction that you desire. If not, then research your beliefs to see if they are obstructing your spiritual view. Make sure those beliefs are factual.

To increase the space for your new found positive beliefs, it is possible that you might need to create room in your spirit to do so. The way to do this is to unbelieve the negative memories of your past, the negative memories of yourself, and the negative memories of as many things that are in your way as possible.

In order to unbelieve something, you must first identify that belief. To do that, you can list your beliefs by writing them out. These are beliefs that have become your gravity in that they've weighed and pulled on your spirit. These are things that you may have said to yourself or someone may have carelessly thrown at you. The following statements are a few examples of negative beliefs that your mind may be subconsciously holding on to: I am fat. I am stupid. Nobody likes me. Nobody wants me. I'm weak. I'm ugly. I am broke. I am an alcoholic. I am a drug addict. The list can go on. You have allowed these negative connotations to take up a majority of space in your belief system, and you've allowed yourself to believe them to be true. Believing in them prevents them from going away and leaves little room for positive beliefs to exist. In order for you to believe in something better, you must first unbelieve these negatives. This will free your spirit and give your mind a chance to focus on positive beliefs.

In order to start the unbelief process, you must plan a series of short-term goals and meet those goals. A positive short-term goal that is met chips away at your spirit's negative beliefs just like short-term goals in fitness chips away body fat. By unbelieving, you are reducing your spiritual obesity. This spiritual exercise technique is extremely powerful for anyone, whether you are struggling in life or extremely successful.

Workouts increase your power of self-belief. Workouts give you the outer and inner strength to do more for yourself, turn your beliefs into a physical reality, and unlock chains in your spirit so that you can have the freedom to excel. If confidence was a muscle, then belief would be its protein. Just as protein is essential in building muscle and maintaining good health, your belief in yourself builds your confidence to do things in life and take bold steps toward accomplishing your dreams. It's better than a leap of faith. It's building a bridge to your dreams. That bridge is made up of hard work, knowledge, and positive people who can assist you along the way.

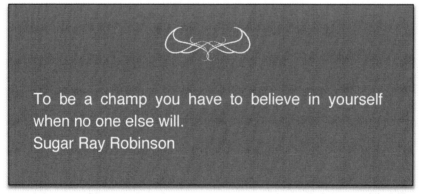

> To be a champ you have to believe in yourself when no one else will.
> Sugar Ray Robinson

When I feel it's necessary to dispel negative beliefs from my clients, I give them a directive to verbally or subconsciously begin repeating positive confirmations instead of negative connotations. For instance, if someone really needs to lose weight, they should tell themselves, "I must lose weight." This leaves no room to dispute that fact. For confidence to change circumstances, they say, "I must strengthen my self-worth," or "I must learn a new trade." To change their social status, they say, "I must love myself first," and "I must get out more and join social circles of like-minded people." "I believe there's someone for me, and I must find them to help in their quest for happiness." "I must improve my physical, mental, and emotional strength." "I must love myself, my beauty, and my attractiveness." "I am capable of achieving great wealth." "I want to live a full, healthy life. Therefore, I must stop drinking or using drugs."

Unbelieve the things that stop you and believe the things that positively motivate you. Through fitness, you'll find the strength and power to overcome your negative beliefs. When you strengthen your positive beliefs, you are taking steps toward success in areas of your life that you previously believed weren't possible.

CHAPTER 5

The Scientific Power Of Attraction

Popular beliefs of attraction have made claims according to laws and the universe. If you behave in a positive manor, positive results will show up in your life. The teachings even goes as far as encouraging people to manifest those dreams and desires into their lives through meditation, to dwell in a mentality that if you can see it, you can be it or have it and to raise your vibration so that you may draw to you those things that match your vibration. Scientists have also confirmed that there is such a thing as an aura. Based on the energy, the amount of electrons and neutrons, your body radiates a field of energy that is detectable by other humans. Your aura can give others an 'indication of your mood and whether you're approachable or not.

But there is also another way to become attractive, a more primal way of drawing people and positive situations into our lives. It's called our pheromones, our body's natural human scent, and in fitness, it's very important to recognize the significance of emitting healthy pheromones and how it contributes to your overall success.

Although scientists and researchers have found direct correlation between pheromones and instinctive attractiveness, most of their research is based on the scent of armpits and some body secretions like tears. These pheromones trigger responses in social settings that can ultimately determine a person's social success or not.

Now, I may not be a scientist, but as a personal trainer, I've worked in close physical proximity to different people on a regular basis while they are sweating and breathing heavily. I easily notice their natural base scent, their pheromones, and I've also noticed as their scent changed or improved so did their social lives. Their lives as a whole became more positive. Therefore, I am convinced that there's a direct correlation between optimal health and people's personal power of attraction.

I have seen people start their fitness journey with toxic scents such as nicotine, alcohol, drugs, and food additives, and during their fitness success, they have eliminated levels of toxic scent from their natural base scent. "You are what you eat," also applies to your scent. What we eat, drink, and ingest becomes a part of our body chemistry, and if the body is toxic, its scent, although not visible, will be sensed or smelled as toxic. The body's base natural scent becomes buried or suppressed, thus inhibiting our truest, most basic source of attractiveness. The good news is that as you begin a life in fitness, you will start peeling back the layers of toxins through the elimination process. The body secretes waste and water, cleansing its entire system and improving and strengthening our immune system which in turn improves the release of our true, and essentially cleaner, pheromones. Our natural based scent is then restored and revealed in its most attractive form.

I like to refer to our personal emission of our natural scent, pheromones, accompanied with your aura as a "micro base scent cloud." When people engage in a fitness lifestyle, including a clean diet, their bodies will restore their micro base scent cloud, improving their success for mating, friendship, and even trust. Engaging your body in exercise, recovery, and proper nutrition will excrete toxins and unwanted chemicals from your body, and at some point, the body recalibrates its immune system and emits a clearer scent cloud, sending it as code to attract favorable opportunities with meeting people. You will find that these people are more attuned to you and will respond with a higher degree of interest for you. This will give you a great advantage in creating a more powerful base of friends, colleagues, business associates, and mates. In today's world, it may not be the water cooler topic in the "laws" of attraction, but our pheromones and aura are our best allies in regards to what makes us attractive.

Accomplishing the task of being physically fit and incorporating the fitness mind into your lifestyle increases your chances for better natural selection in all things in life. Some might see it as luck, but in the fitness mind, it is a process of physical and mental preparation with your whole body, inside and out, that creates positive opportunity.

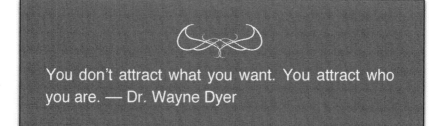

You don't attract what you want. You attract who you are. — Dr. Wayne Dyer

According to the laws of nature, intelligence is our gift for pattern recognition. Science says we are naturally attracted to identifiable patterns, and fitness improves our visual attractiveness. I have seen countless times the effects of improved attraction due to weight loss, increased muscle gain, firmer shapes, etc. The experience of satisfaction for the client is remarkable. I have witnessed a newfound energy of excitement from clients as they joyfully tell me their experiences of attractiveness.

Again, science also tells us that we humans are attracted to outstanding patterns. It's all about patterns and lines—symmetry. As a personal trainer, I have developed a keen eye for physical symmetry. When clients reach their full fit potential, they are not only excited about their weight loss or weight shift from fat to lean muscle, they are excited because their ideal symmetry has become defined and more visible, making them feel more appealing to the eye.

A body slightly enhanced with more muscle can create remarkable patterns, and when we see results, we can't help but have a sense of excitement for ourselves. It's obvious progress. No matter what natural shape and size we were given, the quest for optimal fitness creates attractiveness. The symmetrical lines of the human body cause us to be visually more attracted to other highly symmetrical people. When the body is over or under weight, it sacrifices its natural symmetries, which takes away from its ability to physically attract visually.

Now, with that said, there's nothing wrong with curves or less defined symmetry. Just because science has proven we are attracted to symmetry doesn't mean we aren't attracted to or don't appreciate less definition. Some people are attracted to curves either because they simply like and appreciate something different from their own symmetry or because they associate curvy with sexy, and that's perfectly fine. However, when curvy becomes disproportioned to the body frame or bone structure and puts extra pressure on the heart, the body then looks unhealthy and, therefore, can be perceived as unattractive.

In fitness, anyone's number one priority to achieve personal symmetry should be for health. Achieving great symmetry is a bonus for consistent hard work and dedication, adding to your attractiveness. The desire to improve symmetry will also change your complete outward appearance through a different selection in fashion, beauty products, automobiles, home designs, and everything else associated with this new fascination for patterns.

It's our nature to detect and select particular patterns according to our wants and needs, consciously and subconsciously. This form of attraction is called natural selection. So when you improve your symmetry, you improve your degree of natural selection in relationships, business opportunities, positive situations, and more. Ultimately, it is the conscious effort to put your health first so that good things will follow.

> No matter what anybody says, relationships are based on physical attraction. — Denis Leary

I have found that people, when seeking fitness, are looking to change more than just their physical body. They also want to become more attractive in other aspects of their life.

When you start a fitness program, the beginning might be painful, and you could become frustrated. But after a while, you become stronger and more confident, and your body's desire will connect with your mind and spirit. You'll want more. I've seen it time and time again with my clients. They begin liking what they see, more so, how they feel. They are motivated to continue training to keep up this progress.

The body develops muscle mass from repetition and consistency, so it's a must to continue a fitness lifestyle to achieve these goals. It's also useful to make changes in fitness programming to advance results. In other words, after you've gotten over the first hurdle of getting started, to continue to get better results you must change your routine. You will enjoy the change and the results as well. As too in life, if something isn't getting you the results you desire, it's time to switch it up. You'll be surprised how much fitness will improve your ability to do other things in your life differently.

Once you feel you've tapped into your fitness mind, put your power of attraction to the test. As you've become more fit and begin looking to increase your results, find someone who might be getting that same result you're looking for. Approaching with sincere admiration leaves awkwardness out of the picture and allows for a compliment or questions to flow naturally. Because there is already common ground and you're looking for advice or guidance, most people are willing to oblige a little help at the very least. You will be amazed at the positive response. It's not that your previous way of greeting was bad, but if you were used to the type of response from others where there was no excitement or nothing learned or gained, you may not have been as confident in your ability to attract or create opportunity for a favorable outcome.

If you changed you're greeting, it would be new to you, and the response from others would be new to you as well, causing excitement, which is a display of increased positive energy. A natural attraction to you occurs. That excitement can lead you down a deeper path to opportunity and favorable situations. Changes in fitness routines lead to improved results to become more attractive, and it's all within your reach and capacity. Certain changes in repetitive lifestyle behaviors can turn the mundane into the exciting, the stressful into strength, and the normal into the exceptional.

CHAPTER 6

Gravity And The Power Of Attraction

Newton's law of gravity and motion persist in the fitness atmosphere. Intelligence is a cerebral productive form of gravity. Like the universe, intelligence uses gravity to pull matter into a place of order or chaos. The universe is successful by using systematic patterns to collect matter controlled by gravity. The power of attraction exists because of the negative pull that gravity creates. In order to turn that negative pull into something positive, you must defy gravity intellectually.

Gravity gives us three choices to achieve positivity: 1) Give in to the force of gravity or situation and let it take control, 2) equal the force of gravity or situation and remain of equal space, and 3) summon more force than that which is pulling you and control the way in which you are going. With the first choice, it means you are completely content and do not wish to change anything about your fitness or your life. However, with choices two and three, it takes conditioning and strength for a better or changed life. It takes a conditioning of the mind with mental and spiritual strength and space. If you desire to escape the gravity of a current negative situation, you can use the process of developing a fitness mind to help you escape.

The law of gravity and motion states that with enough velocity, you can escape a particular gravitational pull. We can apply velocity in our lives in different forms, including choosing, moving, doing, building, creating, selling, collecting, paying, seeking, improving, organizing, volunteering, giving, increasing, believing, getting, and so on. Like fitness, becoming stronger in these forces will give you the velocity to move out of the way or escape the orbit of the negative gravity that is consuming you.

The next time you strength train, think about the repetition. It has a positive and a negative side of its motion. The positive side will always require more energy or effort from you to create movement, and that energy is your force, not the force of gravity. Such is life. Build your energy to be stronger than the negative force that is pulling you. The repetition of your strength and the force of gravity, your negative situation, will constantly make you stronger until you can break away from its negative force field or situation.

The power of attraction is a negative force that pulls on you. In order to use it for positive results, you must defy its gravity by being stronger.

I identified how the power of attraction could go wrong by a situation with one of the Incredible 20. He was a hardworking man with an attraction to the entertainment industry. I managed to get him in fantastic shape, which wasn't hard because of his desire to look good for the industry. But it was this uncontrolled desire that lured him away from his true happiness, which was his newly formed family. He was constantly going to sports events and movie premier events, socializing and drinking. In his mind, his attraction seemed right. He justified it as social networking and as a need to get work. But he was also neglecting going home at a reasonable hour to spend time with his family. He was using his new attractiveness on other women and did not attempt to control his allure. On one hand, he had all he desired in his family, but on the other hand, he was enjoying the fringe benefits of the business he loved. The overindulgence was taking a toll, and he wasn't paying attention to the gravity of his situation. He was pulled further and further away from his family and his real responsibilities. Because he did not focus on being stronger than the gravity of this situation, he allowed it to pull him into personal failure. Chaos.

His family left him, and he lost his job. The devastation depleted his energy, and unfortunately, he couldn't continue his training sessions. As a result of all his loss, his personal powers to attract were diminished to the point where it made it hard for him to exist in the very industry that he so desired to be in.

What happened here? My client wasn't prepared mentally to responsibly handle the new level of attraction he was acquiring. Because he did not use greater force than the gravity of his attraction to the entertainment industry, he ended up in a realm outside of everything he had been blessed with and desired. He allowed himself to be lured away from a positive situation he had already created with his family and into a negative situation within his business. The business itself isn't negative, but he didn't participate in it with the strength he would need to make it a positive realm for him and his family.

Again, gravity is a constant attraction. Gravity cannot be controlled, but we can use it to become stronger and apply that strength in our ability to control attraction.

Currently, after years of his absence from me, I have managed to convince him to acquire a fitness mind. While he is headed in the right direction, he is still unfamiliar with where he currently is. He must regain control of his spiritual strength, his sense of self-worth.

In the gym, he is really good at pushing weight around. Physical force comes easily to him, and his body collects strength very well with few aids such as nutritional supplements. But I noticed how unaware he was of his spiritual force. Imagine if he went to the gym and his spiritual force took the place of his physical force that day. It would be as if he was grabbing the weights and throwing them around in the gym, not caring where they landed or who they would hit. That is how his spiritual force is endangering others he cares about, as well as himself, without the proper amount of spiritual self-awareness.

Exercise is only the foundation of health and strength. If you want to achieve your desired goals, you must build from your foundation by improving nutrition and proper rest for recovery. In the gym, the essentials are gravity, matter, and motion. The universe works with gravity, matter, and motion, and so too does life work from gravity, matter, and motion.

Success can be duplicated and recreated, but no two successes are identical. Just like people. The power of attraction in the universe, gravity, uses the same systems and the same matter to develop galaxy after galaxy, solar system after solar system, planet after planet. And yet, although similar, no two galaxies, solar systems, or planets are identical.

In the fitness world, we use the same systems, same machines, and same routines to develop similar but different results in each person. The universe has demonstrated to us that the same system can generate different patterns and different results. In the law of attraction, the power to change is the objective. In fitness, changing your routine will increase your results. In health, changing your diet will improve your health. In finances, changing the way you handle your life can improve your wealth. In happiness, changing the way you feel spiritually can make you happier.

If you don't like something, change it. If you can't change it, change your attitude. — Maya Angelou

As a personal trainer, I encourage change, and with every new client, I am prepared to change their lives. You can use your power in the law of attraction to change your inner self just as much as you can use it to attract external success into your life.

Respecting gravity is what I believe my client had to learn, which is not only the gravitational pull on earth but also the gravity or heaviness that pulls on the heart and mind, when you try to focus on something currently important but your mind reverts back to a previous situation. You can put your results in jeopardy when you lose focus during an exercise and miss your mark or goal. In the case of my client, he lost focus of his home. He let gravity pull his heart away from the needs of his family. He did not use his internal energy to thrust away from the party lifestyle. He did not move away from that negative pulling force that eventually caused spiritual, mental, and physical pain.

Gravity pulls on us from the time we are born. We are in a continuous effort to move through earth's gravitational pull in our body and in our mind. Like in the gym where we use mental and physical effort to get through a workout, we also use mental and physical effort to get through life. If you can learn how to detect your heart's gravity and strengthen yourself to mentally thrust through situational gravity, it will help you succeed in any environment in life. The body can only lift and hold so much weight at a time before it has to set it down, rest, recover, and try again. The mind can only hold so many active memories at a time before it has to set them aside, rest, and recover.

In the universe, stars burst, sending the matter into space to be collected by gravity again and again. In the gym, you exercise, recover, and do the exercise again and again. In life, your situations burst and distribute energy, which is recovered and used again and again. That's gravity creating attraction. So in essence, you can never fail. You only have to start again. Like the universe, we are built to collect and release energy. When you release energy according to your work ethic, your personal universe expands by way of promotion, finances, opportunities, and fortune.

These are keys to using earth's negative force of gravity for positive results. The body moves according to the law of attraction. The mind thinks according to the law of attraction in the context of the negative power of the universe, gravity. You must generate your own positive results. To believe is to thrust into gravity or to leave from a previous state of mind in the direction of something else, to use energy in order to sustain a direction mentally, spiritually, or physically. If you allow your mind to focus on the patterns of your fitness workouts, you can learn to use these observations and findings to further understand and succeed in life.

Use fitness to attract positive thoughts into your mind. One of the keys to success is positive thinking. It is impossible to succeed without thinking and operating positively. During your workouts, your body and mind release a large portion of your collected energy. That released energy is coded with your thought patterns and meditations of your expectations in life. That's why it is important to focus on good things returning to you for the hard work you've put in your workouts. When you have completed your workout session, your depleted body and mind will need replenishing. The body's recovery system will want healthy and positive things put back in it to replace what it has released. This is a good time to think positive, beneficial, healthy thoughts and take in helpful information for yourself and eat healthy foods.

As your body replenishes energy, it will pull to you positive things based on your coded energy. At some point, these things will appear in your realm for your using. If you are keen to your coded energy, you will see them as they appear. Think of it as a more modern way of mediation or prayer. You are not just using your words and thoughts and feelings as in conventional prayer. You are using your mind's words, your heart's feelings, and your body's energy collectively being released into earth's gravity field. I'll label this as "modern turbo prayer meditation." During each workout, you are keeping your mind and heart and the effort of your workout focused on the return of positive things, and you should congratulate yourself for the time spent and the work you put in. This is the easiest way to start the process of building a stronger, positive self. This practice will improve your outlook for success in life.

Your body can manifest your success in fitness if you attract your senses to what's happening to your body and equate it to what's happening in your life emotionally, spiritually, and financially: lose weight, lose emotional depression; gain strength, gain spiritual confidence; meet your fitness goals, meet your financial goals; lose body fat, lose financial debt. The correlations will help you condense your focus and behavior patterns, thus giving you another perspective to use to your advantage.

CHAPTER 7

The Energy Of Fitness

The energy of fitness is a transformation of energy that radiates from your fitness results to the results of life's elements. In your fitness mind, your fitness energy can act as the sun does with the earth, creating, sustaining, and growing things that matter in your life and making your life stronger. Your fitness energy can increase the value of your dreams, giving you the energy to grow your dreams into reality.

Your fitness energy can increase your motivation for your goals in life. Accomplishing worthy goals takes a tremendous amount of discipline and energy. Developing the discipline to build your fitness energy only better prepares you for achieving your worthy goals. Those that reach higher successes in life usually resort to fitness in order to have the energy to keep up with their success. That's why you'll find that a large percent of highly successful people with demanding careers have a personal trainer. It's a maintenance mechanism for their health to keep up with their work and lifestyle.

Your fitness energy can give you the light to see your way through dark times. In other words, those who have been illuminated in the fitness mind, meaning they've achieved strength and understanding of gravity in the mind, body, and spirit, have learned to see a way through darkness. In a fitness mind, you have better probability to look for the light, a way to succeed, or a way to win, whereas people who are in a negative state of mind will probably seek more negativity, which is gravity dominating your mind. Your fitness energy can give you the power to grow out of your current place in life. If your life needs growth, fitness can give you the energy to do so. It gives you the strength to move at a different speed in life. The energy of fitness causes you to streamline your necessities for success.

During personal training sessions, I often overrule someone's desire to rest or stop. That's because I am focused on knowing the capability of each person I train. I know the body. So while their mind is stuck on the discomfort of the task, my mind is focused on them completing it. A person with a fitness mind understands this and pushes through the difficulties and discomforts to complete the task. Your fitness energy can give you the ability to create great things from the simplest things. In the fitness world, people are surprised when I assign a certain light weight to their exercise. They assume that they need more to get results. After I guide them through the proper technique, their muscles are screaming with success. Life is that way too. It doesn't take a lot to make a success, but it does take knowledge, effort, and technique. Those three things are life's gym.

The energy from fitness can give you clear focus as a single ray of light on an object. The single sun ray can change the composition of an object such as making a tree bear fruit. When you apply your energy to a situation or goal, your focus allows you clarity to make decisions and changes and take chances for the best or intended result. If your fitness energy has the ability to gain muscle and lose weight, that same applied energy can cause fruitfulness in other parts of your life.

Simple can be harder than complex. You have to work harder to get your thinking clean to make it simple. It's worth it in the end because once you get there you can move mountains. — Steve Jobs

Your fitness energy will also increase your inner courage, which helps you make decisions you wouldn't ordinarily make. Gaining more energy from fitness is like increasing the power of your car. Courage is part of what's under the hood of your car. Sure, you have a car that can go two hundred miles an hour, but are you going to ever use its full potential? Or are you going to be the one that takes the steps to fully be a part of what it was designed to do, to learn how to drive at that speed and take it to a legal race track and experience its potential? Sounds like fun, doesn't it? If you've done that, you know the limits of a car. You know how it feels at high speeds. The adrenaline rush is exhilarating. Now, would you do this on a regular basis? Probably not, but the point is that you've proved and acquired an understanding of what it feels like to perform at that car's full potential. You will have developed a deeper respect and understanding of that vehicle. In applying this to a fitness mind and the energy of fitness, you should use your mind and body for all its designed to do. Only then will this lifestyle change and the experience be worth it.

As a personal trainer, I see people engage in fitness for the first time and start off doing too much, trying to accomplish in one fitness session what takes months, even years, to accomplish. They jump into it not knowing the length of the journey. They didn't consult with a professional before beginning. I can almost instantly see the ones who will succeed and the ones who will not.

I've been in the fitness business for a long time, so I understand that it takes time to develop fitness energy. The body doesn't respond over one night but over many nights. However, you can start feeling the chemical changes the body is going through and how it causes you to start feeling good about working out almost instantly. Each workout adds positive data to the pleasure center of the brain to be used for other elements of your life. Starting a journey for success in other elements of your life is no different.

It is best to seek the knowledge of a professional in your area of interest to chart a good understanding of how long it will take to reach your desired goals before you start your quest. A professional personal trainer will know what equipment and exercises to use to help you get in shape. You should know exactly what tools you will need to succeed. Also, it is key to start off by accomplishing tasks you can handle. Too much can lead to discouragement and failure.

If you're just starting out, begin with attainable goals, or if you have plateaued, find new attainable goals. When you succeed, you recruit positive energy into your situation. Your energy level increases, and greater time and resistance are needed to keep increasing your fitness energy and success. The more you get in shape, the faster your results will come and the more your energy will accumulate. Again, still accomplish tasks you can handle. As long as you increase after a set goal, you will sustain and increase your strength and levels of accomplishments. As in life when you start achieving results, you will add to those results with growth, and your energy will continue to expand.

I have seen people push the limit, trying to go beyond their capabilities in an attempt to reach a currently unobtainable goal. They end up getting injured, which is a setback. There is greed in fitness like every other element of life. When you avoid the fitness greed, you avoid injury.

The greatest reward for building fitness energy is in the active quality of life you will have for many years. In saying that, if you use these correlations with the other areas and elements of your life, you will experience a continued growth and a quality of life that will be superb.

In time, your fitness energy will shine through your total self and attract positive things into your life. Your fitness energy will illuminate your presence. When you exercise on a constant basis, the energy that you build shows on your outer shell. How? When you increase your fitness level, you are strengthening your heart and lungs. Thus, you are pumping more blood through your veins per second than you did before on a regular basis. Because of this increased blood flow, your skin radiates a particular glow more than people who don't exercise on a fitness level. This is true at any age. In essence, you are hot! Your body is more thermogenic than the average sedentary person. Because of this, you develop a slight illumination that is noticeably attractive. Unfortunately, most people never figure this out when they look at someone and can't explain why they are attracted to that person or drawn to look at or speak to him or her. That slight glow speaks healthy and strong. For women, it can even be better than makeup because we are attracted to natural, healthy looks. This particular part of our biology exists primarily for signaling attraction that all is functioning well and giving an appealing, warm appearance.

As a fitness professional working in private gyms, it's easy to observe the changes of at least fifty to sixty people a day exercising. I see the before and after in real time. I see the slight changes and drastic changes in people through time. But what's most astounding is that I've noticed an actual fitness glow. It's not the flushed look one might have after a workout session but an aura of light that proceeds them. It's a healthy glow that comes from within them and radiates strength from the contained positive energy that they acquired through fitness. I also see the attraction that it brings and how people react to this glow. Those with a fitness mind understand that when people look at them, the fitness glow is one of the reasons why.

At first, when you are new to an exercise regimen the glow will only last about three hours. But in time, after you have developed fitness energy, your glow will last for days as long as you stay consistent with your workout sessions. The longer you stay in fitness, the longer your glow. Developing your fitness energy is the ultimate self-illumination formula.

When you go to the gym to exercise, meet with your trainer, or do group exercises, you acquire a particular and a certain amount of positive energy for that day. The attraction that you feel when you are drawn to go workout is the same particular positive magnetism that people feel when they are drawn to you. It is a sense of positive power, strength, well-being, profitable direction, and purpose. In essence, fitness gives you the energetic power of leadership should you accept it in any of its forms. Imagine yourself as a glowing entity that has just recently left its source of light but still shines as you carry out life on your path. The energy of fitness radiates on and within you.

Your fitness energy can potentially give you the stamina to out work anyone else and become a champion of your choosing. It is the continuous pursuit of physical fitness that will give you the insight of a fitness mind. Using this energy can give you the power to think and make clear decisions faster than the average person, giving you a clear advantage with success. And most importantly, the energy of fitness will give you the ability to look and live better longer.

CHAPTER 8

Fitness Knowledge And Your Potential

Fitness knowledge is not just about learning different exercises and routines to help you get in shape. It is also learning about oneself through fitness to gain an insight of what you are made of inside and out. It's about spiritually bonding together your body and your mind to work toward a common goal. It is about digging deep into yourself and becoming truly aware of what exists within you and understanding how to use it. As Albert Einstein tells us, "Education is not the learning of facts, but the training of the mind." In other words, information or data only becomes knowledge when you apply what you've learned. Therefore, knowledge is education, application, and the ability to understand how it all works together. So when your eyes and mind realize how much you've learned or can learn about yourself through fitness, you harness power of your potential. This knowledge will spark your motivation to use it as often as possible, becoming a perpetual state of the fitness mind.

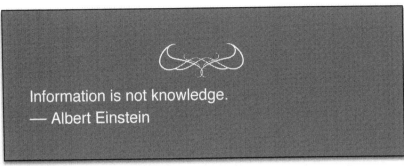

Information is not knowledge.
— Albert Einstein

By the mere fact that you're reading this book means that you are seeking insight to increase your speed toward success in becoming completely fit. The mind is truly the best place to start. Not preparing yourself mentally is more detrimental than people might think because once you are completely knowledgeable about yourself and your capabilities, you are more likely to stay the course to continuous improvement. By strengthening and applying your fitness education, you are already on your way to minimizing negativity and bringing about maximum positivity in your life as a whole. Soon, you'll see your work habits sharpen, your setbacks decrease, and your results increase. Your fitness mind will give you an inner ability to focus your energy and not waste time, giving you more time in between triumphs to enjoy life.

It may not be easy to achieve making all the first steps to become fit, but don't let the weight of past failures slow you down. Seeking professional assistance could prove helpful. Even if it's just a consultation for direction, it's worth it. You're worth it.

You also must dispel the fear and negative beliefs you have set as knowledge for yourself as mentioned in Chapters 1 and 2. It's the job of trainers, coaches, and fitness professionals to empower those they are working with to accomplish a task, decreasing the opportunity for negative thoughts and self-doubt to dwell in the mind.

Learning the various exercises and how to best use equipment for your age, weight, and ability will also be helpful. I've seen so many people use equipment over and over and never achieve the results they want because they're using it improperly. So if you can consult a professional, please do. Again, the fitness mind is never without applying effort for improvement, including knowledge of oneself, to strengthen and add positive dimensions to your life. As with success in any pursuit, you must continue to educate yourself if you want success in fitness.

Imagine a track and field athlete, a high jumper who's never attempted the high jump, but is learning for the first time. A coach has the information and understands how it should be done and how to teach it. The athlete listens to the coach and immediately understands what the coach is saying and has the physical knowledge to carry out the jump. The athlete understands how his body moves and can move. He can physically turn the information he learned from the coach into physical application. He understands how to do something and then does it. Fitness has put him in tune with his ability. His first attempts at the high jump will probably not be perfect, but he'll continue fine-tuning his mechanics to accomplish it with or without his coach. This is how fitness knowledge works to implement information into results. Education plus application equals experience that ultimately gives you knowledge. You can be very informed about something, but only until you do it are you completely knowledgeable. Now that you're educating yourself, your knowledge in other areas of your life can also benefit from your efforts. The momentum has begun.

When you exercise, you are doing something so incredibly positive for your body and mind, and they want to reward you for your efforts. Again, your journey to success won't be overnight, and anything worth having isn't truly appreciated unless earned. But once you've reached a level of fitness knowledge and energy, your potential will grow exponentially. However, the sooner you start, the quicker you'll reap the rewards. Your positive energy will radiate, and you'll automatically receive favorable energy in return.

You will know your fitness energy has been activated when you not only have a euphoric feeling of being unconquerable but you're also motivated by great ideas and possibly new dreams to achieve. Because your fitness energy causes you to access a larger portion of your brain than normal energy, it is similar to being able to unlock encrypted files of information on your computer. You can use this fitness knowledge for just about anything. You can build a business, create art, write a book, run for public office, find a better job learn a new language ,and more. Your fitness knowledge is a combination of what you learned and how you can use that new level of energy to move your life in a powerful direction. In essence, if you continue to develop a fitness mind, you can use it to maximize your experience to what life has to offer.

When you're ready to access your mind for productivity, like with exercise, you want to warm up before you do the bulk of your heavy or intense exercising. Within a four- to six-hour time frame after working out, you want to use that fresh flow of blood to mentally sort and produce results pertaining to your personal goals. Doing this consistently will give you a tremendous boost in results. Your thought processes will be more streamlined, and your inner vision will be clearer. The more frequently you do this, the more thorough your results will be. Eventually, things that took months will take weeks, and things that took weeks will take days. Using fitness before facing life's goals and challenges is the greatest app the mind could ever hope for.

To start gaining these types of benefits from you workouts, start with something small or simple. After a workout session, try doing a short recovery period about an hour or so long. Get yourself ready to do something positive, creative, or productive in a way that will lead to fulfilling your dreams. The added energy from your workout will give you an advantage in achieving that goal. That is because your mind has just recently received a reward signal to the pleasure center of your brain. Also, your adrenaline levels are at a peak, and your blood is full of positive hormones. But timing is key. At this time, being full of fitness energy and working toward other goals will draw or attract people and events into your efforts in favor of you.

> Should you find yourself in a constantly leaking boat, the energy devoted to changing vessels is likely to be more productive than energy devoted to patching leaks.
> — Warren Buffet

Be smart and feel the power of your fitness energy! Be aware of what you are doing when you are fresh into your fitness energy each day. Target good productivity. Avoid letting it dwindle on mindless and meaningless things. Avoid the fitness vacuum. The fitness vacuum, internet vacuum, success vacuum, and paper vacuum are all voids people fall into by repeating the same thing over and over without any thought as to why they are doing it. This process diminishes energy instead of building energy.

As a personal trainer, I have learned to improve on human adaptation. Because the body adapts to its environment, the need for change is constant if you want to improve your results. In health, there is nothing wrong with doing the same thing over and over if it is safe and healthy. But if you want to improve your physical results, you will have to change variables. In life, every level of success hits a wall. If you want to continue to grow, you will have to use the knowledge you've gained about yourself and not be afraid to apply it toward a new way of life.

CHAPTER 9

Social Fitness

Social fitness is important in success because it is necessary to communicate with others in order to prosper. Strength is an improvable value in fitness. Some are more socially strong than others, but that doesn't mean that one cannot become stronger or better at social behavior.

In the fitness mind, to be social is to take in the energy of others. But in order to take in the energy of others, you must exert your own energy into this field. In other words, when you go to the gym or your fitness group, you are surrounded by people with a common goal to be in shape and to excel. When you observe others in fitness, it gives you feedback on yourself. It gives you insight on your own accomplishments in the gym or fitness group. You see people doing certain exercises and the results they have obtained doing them, and you start to do those exercises too. Whether you are aware of it or not, it gives you added energy and motivation to do better and perform outside of your own current abilities.

This creates progress. In life, your social world can be the same. Being surrounded by goal oriented people will give you the same added energy to perform higher, thus giving you feedback on yourself. In the fitness mind, one of the driving forces is the need to improve, grow, strengthen, and move forward. Creating a strong social network can accelerate your chances for success. It is a universal factor that human energy needs other human energy to feed off of. Those that embrace this need improve their chances for success.

As a personal trainer, I witness over and over people's need to interact with both familiar and unfamiliar people. In a world where individuality is dominant, the quest for social connection remains high. If you look into your life or the lives of others, you'll see behavior patterns that are directly connected to our social environment, which can be contributed to failure or success.

Social media is an amazing tool, but it's really face-to-face interaction that makes a long-term impact. — Felicia Day

In the fitness mind, the better shape you're in mind, body, and spirit, the more desire you have for healthy social stimulation. When you work out for physical improvement and better health, your body releases hormones that satisfy the pleasure center of the brain. Social stimulation effects the same pleasure center of the brain, creating spiritual and emotional motivation and the need to repeat the process of social activity for human satisfaction. Of course, we have different motivations for social stimulation, but they all lead to the need for human satisfaction. Fitness gives us a deeper connection to social stimulation, a stronger need for human interaction. This increased need for human interaction puts you closer to success.

In this day and age of digital social communication, we can become socially out of shape, alienating ourselves from the very thing we are looking for on the Internet, the developing stories of friends as if it is the evening news. There's no turning back from this type of social interactivity, but there has to be a balance. In fitness, you cannot get in shape sitting on your couch looking at a fitness video on TV. In the same way, you cannot become socially strong or increase your success unless you physically meet people who have similar goals.

If you want to be socially fit, just as in physical fitness, you must continue to try and learn so that you can become better. It is in our human nature to continuously grow and improve upon our social existence, but some unconsciously get stuck in a place and time. They experience a constant gravity pull, giving just enough energy to stay in that one place. A person who is socially unfit is a person who uses the same approach and gets the same undesired or failed result. For example, if someone is constantly unsuccessful with introducing themselves to people, they must push through the gravity of fear. They must find the courage and confidence in themselves to take their greeting a step further. They must use the information they've gathered to create small talk, press on to engage in more weighted conversation, and then move the talks to their desired results from the social interaction.

When you're approaching something differently for the first time, that anxious tension is normal, but it's surmountable. That nervous energy is the very energy you'll use to break through the gravity, giving you an opportunity to achieve your goal. Push yourself to socialize. If you're hesitant or find being shy to be a personality factor in your quest to become more sociable, you might press forward in open activity classes, group sporting events, etc. Social websites have become a powerful tool in assisting people to connect to one another based on similar interest. And while they add value to the social environment, they cannot touch the human spirit the way real human social contact can.

In the fitness mind, you can exercise at home using a fitness video, and you will get results. But if you want the real fitness experience, a more powerful and spiritual approach, exercising with others around or having a trainer will enhance the quality of your life and give you outlets for more prosperous opportunities both for fun and for financial growth.

> To succeed you will soon learn, as I did, the importance of a solid foundation in the basics of education: literacy, both verbal and numerical, and communication skills. — Alan Greenspan

When you go to the gym, there is a social way to conduct yourself, which is pretty standard across the nation. You must use the equipment a certain way, and there are signs that remind you. There is a certain gym behavior that most people adapt to when moving to the flow of the gym. Those that capitalize on the flow of the gym get more done, and their results are better.

There are very few places in this world that give us the opportunity to physically share things on a consistent basis. Sharing gym equipment requires us to socially interact in a sharing manner. This is a good place to practice and improve your social skills for both normal and highly skilled social people. You can leave the gym knowing that you not only worked out your body but also your social skills.

External self-observation, in my opinion, is one of our most powerful habits and helps us with our people skills. It's another area where we can build integrity. When someone comes to the gym and starts training to get in shape, they are doing so to change and improve their body and their feelings about their body. But in order to change your body, you must also be conscious of your eating habits. Likewise, if you want to change the perception that people have of you, you must not only change the outside but improve the inside, including your social skills. One can never cease to improve in this area.

In the gym, when people are about to start an exercise, I usually see a pause as if to go in thought about something. Now, in my fitness mind, I would love to think they are visualizing their exercise and how perfect they can make each repetition, gearing their mind up to control their muscles every inch of every rep, and how they can squeeze every inch of results out of that set. And in return, that energy spent will return something favorable. But I know that is not always the case.

In the social world, people do the same thing. Some people think before they speak, and some people don't think before they speak. They just say whatever is on their mind, no matter what, only controlling themselves half the time they communicate. But people who think before they speak can achieve much better results per word, thus achieving success in conveying their message.

I think it speaks highly of you when you think before you approach your workout. Contemplation develops focus, and focus summons strength. Soon you will have developed a culture of using proper technique, which is almost a guarantee of intended results.

As a personal trainer who has practically lived his life in the gym, I have seen people at their best and their not so best. I have seen people who give their all every time, and I have seen people fake exercising just to look attractive and draw attention. While they might look great doing that perfect exercise with two pounds, their results come up empty. Perception of these people might be as they've hoped. In the social world, people say and do things that bring them negative attention or undesired results if any at all. That's fine if you want no results in life, but if you do, speak and conduct yourself, your exercise, and your life with purpose for intentions of getting excellent results.

The more effort you give in being socially positive, the more favorable opportunities and results will come your way. Gravity pulls on everything. But when you push through gravity, you get what you want, and you go in the direction you want to go.

When lifting weights, your body gets stronger by its ability to push weight through gravity. The more you push a desired weight through gravity, the more weight you can push through gravity. Being socially strong is similar in that the more effort you give being socially positive, the more positive results you obtain.

I've had clients who have become socially overwhelmed. The weight of their world has pushed them down. Being socially strong or having good people skills thrusts you through life's gravity, pushing you in the direction that you want to go. Everyone's social muscle is different, but everyone can improve and strengthen it.

The stronger your social muscle, the more of life's weight you can push through gravity.

There have been clients who have stopped working out for long periods of time. Some come back. When they do, I have to start from the basics and build them back up again, but the results come back, sometimes even quicker than before. Refreshing social skills will do the same thing in life. It's like giving your personality a tune up.

The heart endures many challenges, including social pressure. But just like getting in shape for short or long distance cardio, you can also train your heart to endure many other physical challenges that come from relationships and everyday life. The way to do this is to practice deep breathing just as you would practice breathing when you are doing physical cardio aerobics or any other cardiovascular exercise.

Take deep breaths and blow out to catch your wind and to regulate the rest of your body by letting yourself relax as you exert force and energy. But more importantly, when you are performing cardio, you perform better when you let go of all things in your mind other than controlling your body in the present moment. You give up thinking about things outside of your body. You only focus on your breathing, arm movement, leg movement, and what steps are directly in front of you. All other things have been placed aside.

In your social world, you can use the same principles to accomplish a tough task. Most people view stress as a symptom of mental pressure. I see stress as your natural senses elevating your body's metabolism or revving your engine, so to speak, for performance. It forces your mind to keep thinking about something because it wants you to do something about it. During your stress moments, your body is in performance mode to increase the ability of your mind to do things more efficiently and to not miss details.

When you do something directly connected to what is stimulating your stress, your body takes its foot off the pedal once you have done something about the situation.

Stress, to me, is your subconscious preparing you for action. When you don't do anything about what's causing the stress, your body can develop problems. It's like redlining a car's rpm for nothing. We have conditioned our society to think of stress as an illness that needs medicine instead of a signal that means perform. However, if you can change your perception of stress and condition yourself to handle pressure, you'll be able to act with integrity in any situation, including social settings

CHAPTER 10

Strengthen Your Focus

When we attempt to accomplish any physical task, whether it is lifting weights, doing cardio, hiking, or enduring a long distance run or walk, we must summon a great source of energy called strength. If we know going in that the physical and challenging task will end soon and the benefits will be long-lasting and satisfying, we will be more likely to approach the task with pleasure And once we're done and have rested, we've gained more strength for the next attempt. Building strength is a gift that keeps giving. So too in life we must use our mental source of strength, our spiritual source of strength, and our emotional source of strength to accomplish our goals or to overcome barriers between us and our dreams. In most instances, the process of becoming strong will not happen overnight but in time and with consistent focus.

Have you ever tried to lift or pull weight that was too heavy and uncomfortable for you at first, and you had to adjust the weight to a heaviness that was possible? It becomes obvious very quickly that your body hasn't generated enough strength to lift that weight. Your strength isn't quite there yet. However, when you put yourself through a series of lighter repetitions, you will find that your body has started generating more energy and power, and after a short rest, you are able to move the heavier weight. You might even finish stronger, lifting more than you anticipated. This is where focus becomes your asset to completing anything. It is the moment when you can actually witness yourself summoning that great source of energy, your strength to pull you through the motion. The benefits of this process far exceed just accomplishing a rep. It allows you the belief that you can accomplish anything if you remain focused, especially through the uncomfortable times.

Every time you leave the gym, you should have the feeling that you can conquer the world. There are lots of different ways that you can motivate yourself both spiritually and mentally to conquer the world, but nothing holds more truth than leaving the gym with a fitness mind.

Facing your fears, untruths about yourself, or challenges facing you, there is nothing you can't work through. There are always moments when we find ourselves in compromising positions, but it's also the place where we find our strength. In this strength, your integrity will come into play, the truth you believe about yourself will show, and your focus will determine your action. Will you give in? Will you cower? Or will you muster through and summon all you have to persevere? Just like fitness will make you stronger with repetition, so too will repeating this process make your spirit and your mind stronger.

Fitness helps you streamline your focus in ways that start from a subconscious level. Thinking success in the gym can permeate in your everyday life, and succeeding in fitness can lead to succeeding in life. Being in the best shape of your life can lead to being in the best financial situation in your life. Every time you put in a successful workout, you can put in a successful day's work to gain access to your hopes and dreams. Your physical fitness is more than just your health; it gives you access to new paths to a more fruitful and fulfilling future.

I see people all the time with unlimited potential who leave the gym having harnessed so much power, summoned so much strength, yet once outside the gym, they let all that knowledge of fitness gains go to waste. They don't use the principals their body just taught them, or they simply throw their progress away by living destructive or contradictory lifestyles. I am not saying everyone who comes out of the gym should live a perfect life or have that capability, but it certainly puts everyone at an advantage in life. So to not maximize the benefits would be a waste of energy and strength. Why wouldn't you have it all if it's available to you? If you incorporate your heart and mind for fitness and your results from fitness into the rest of your life as principles for success, you will be fulfilled.

I encourage you to become a cerebral astronomer for a moment. Imagine your brain as a cerebral galaxy, meaning it is full of ideas in memory that are waiting to be discovered. The unlimited information that your body has stored in your brain gives you the ability to find choice after choice to explore, just as an astronomer can find star after star to explore. It helps to understand your brain in this manner because a large part of it has not been tapped or discovered. Putting your brain back into a learning phase gives you the opportunity to expand your horizons or increase the value of your life and become more successful. Just as an astronomer seeks to learn about the possibilities of a new star, you can seek to learn about the possibilities from a new choice.

The knowledge of fitness is already written into your body once you start the process of exercising for better health. If you focus on this knowledge, it will give you access and ways to accomplish your dreams. Many great and successful people have used the knowledge of fitness to gain access to personal success, financial success, social success, spiritual success, and success in many other things.

Strength is only needed in finite amounts of time. You must never fail to use your strength in all aspects of your life when the time arises. Bypassing the opportunities to do so will diminish your chances for success.

To gain strength through focus, we must also learn how important rest is to the equation. Work and rest reward one another. Too much of either causes imbalance, and focus is near impossible.

Science has discovered that our brain naturally goes through cycles with peaks and valleys of work and rest. When you fall asleep, you enter REM sleep after about ninety minutes of non-REM sleep, and you continue to cycle in this way throughout the night.

As it turns out, our brains and bodies go through similar cycles during the day. Our heart alternates between beating and resting; our lungs inhale and exhale; our entire body is pulsing off and on, and our brain is participating in this cycling as well. Sleep researchers have found the same oscillations from higher to lower states of alertness during the day.

To maximize your output, it is vital that you honor these peaks and valleys by balancing concentration with relaxation. Equate the forms and systems of your fitness experiences to life. Life is a workout. When you set out to achieve a particular goal in fitness, you should have a plan. In this plan, you must include rest because execution does not guarantee everything will go as planned. You'll need the ability to rethink and refocus then push through. You will reach each set of goals as long as you are cognoscente of your strength and applying it to press on.

In fitness, every workout requires a certain amount of time. There's a window of seconds before the muscle should retract in order to gain strength. If you start too late, you've lost momentum. You are back at square one. With fitness, there's little room for procrastination. If you want to achieve goals, the more focused you are on time, the faster you'll get to success.

To achieve your personal goals, every task should only take a certain amount of time. So, when you start a task, don't leave room for procrastination. When you finish a workout, you replenish, rest, and plan the next workout. But you start your workout after you've recovered from the last.

In life, you must recover from each task to be fresh for the next task. Running yourself ragged won't lead to crisp results, especially after you've reached the top of your mountain. Routine workouts are good as long as there is progress. But when your progress flat lines, you need to change your routine. In life, if you want to improve your success, you must refocus your plans.

There is no fitness workout without exercises. In life, there are exercises we have to endure when challenges arise. Some people look at challenges or setbacks as a test, and in many ways, they are tests. In the fitness mind, it is an exercise. It is something you must finish if you want to get stronger. You must use effort and inner strength, not guess and wonder. The more life exercises you do, the better you get at taking on tasks or problems.

In a workout routine, you exercise in sets. In life, you accomplish goals in sets. When you work five days in a week, that would be five reps. When you get paid for that week and you make a deposit, that would be one set. You get stronger with each set, meaning when you make a deposit, you properly recover by not overindulging after your work or workouts. When you meet your recovery goal and add to it, your funds grow stronger. The stronger you are, the more you can do and achieve without delay. In the fitness mind, we call it gains. When you develop a fitness mind, your gains will ultimately be determined not just by your strength but by your focus and your ability to tackle any task with your full attention.

CHAPTER 11

Ancient Health & Fitness: Your Right To Be Fit

There's no doubt our bodies were made to achieve great form, no matter your shape or size, but did you ever think being physically fit was a privilege? In ancient times, many rulers banned the practice of enhancing one's body for personal health or appearance. To be fit and agile was considered a form of armor to protect and defend oneself against an enemy. Ancient rulers also understood the power and might a person felt from gaining strength, which is why they only allowed a chosen few to undergo physical training. Leaders, soldiers, and protectors of the nation were to be well trained and maintain a high standard of physical fitness. However, lay persons, servants, and slaves were prohibited from doing anything to enhance their physical capacity so much so that being caught exercising for any reason was a death sentence. Keeping these people average or weak was a preventative measure to avoid outbreaks of freedom fighting and kept the peace. So unless you were part of the chosen few and using your physical fitness for the good of the nation, that privilege was outlawed.

Today, gyms are open twenty-four hours, and there's no limit or law against physical fitness. Yet 70% of all adults, seventeen and older, in the United States are overweight or obese. Free will and opportunity has unfortunately caused many to take physical training for granted. Many have been seduced by the food industries, which further cripples their human instinct for fitness. But all is not lost. If we can again recall that reason, purpose, or obligation that motivates us toward better health, the history of ancient health and fitness can help us exercise our privilege and further our goals.

No man has the right to be an amateur in the matter of physical training. It is a shame for a man to grow old without seeing the beauty and strength of which his body is capable.
— Socrates

When Herbert Spencer, an English philosopher, coined the phrase "survival of the fittest," he was speaking of the evolution and progression of man through survival and reproduction. Today, the term "fitness" implies just that. It is to physically and biologically progress the body to be greater and stronger and to reproduce a race of humans smarter and more resilient than the last. So what we do today will be written in our DNA and passed on as we reproduce. That includes our eating habits and our health and fitness regimens.

We are to be stronger, smarter, and wiser than our predecessors, so it baffles me when I hear of young men and women dying before their parents because of poor health choices. Somewhere there has been a disconnect. Sure, food sources have changed, and technology has made almost everything effortless. But we were made to adapt and continue to improve our way of life, including what we eat and how we maintain our physique. We should be cognizant of this, not only for personal reasons but also for the health and wellness of the predisposed generations to come.

It's in our DNA to be fit if only we will allow ourselves to listen to instincts of the nomadic years of human existence, a time when humans had to maintain a strong and healthy body in order to survive. Nomadic people were able to walk great distances to avoid bad weather, and they had the strength to hunt and gather heavy foods and materials for life. Self-reliance made them more and more resilient.

Until this day, man's continuous strides in health and fitness improvements provided strength and improved thought and intelligence to start building shelter to defy weather and preserve food. With some of man's greatest achievements in automation, technology, advanced engineering, artificial intelligence, and medicine, we have come to rely less on physical activity that used to be mandatory for survival. It is now up to us to make the choice to balance all the modern day conveniences with physical exercise.

In the beginning of the agricultural age, the plow required physical strength to operate. This device gave the users a tremendous advantage in life from those who did not use the plow for food and trade. Those who used the plow were stronger and lived longer because their bodies grew stronger and more resistant to disease, whereas those who started relying on the plowers for food production did not get that exercise unless there job was just as physical. That in turn led to a growing number of sedentary dwellers and caused a number of diseases, including diabetes and heart disease. However, in some ancient civilizations, the development of organized physical activities was formed to combat sedentary lives and cut down the growing number of diseases caused by a lack of activity.

In China, emperors implemented organized activities such as kung fu, gymnastics, badminton, and wrestling. The health benefit paid off with increased productivity of workforces in that era.

However, in India, it was frowned upon to participate in physical activities because it was thought to interfere with the beliefs of Buddhism and Hinduism, which put the spirit above all and sacrificed the body's condition. As a result, the human spirit of the people found a way to exercise without appearing to exercise. It was disguised as prayer and relaxing meditation. This form of exercise is now called yoga and incorporates the mind, body, and spirit.

During the Persian Empire, fitness was encouraged in society from a young age to develop and maintain a strong military force. However, after the rise of the Persian Empire, complacency, corruption, and greed led to a decrease in the demand for fitness and ultimately led to the fall of the empire.

History has shown that the need for exercise has mutated in our human development, turning it into a need and desire for summoning more inner strength and a more positive life.

No other culture has drastically changed the incorporation of fitness into a lifestyle more than the Greeks, particularly the Spartans and the Athenians. So it's no wonder why films and television shows emulate the statuesque figures of men and women of this time.

Although the Spartans viewed fitness as a way to have supremacy in battle, it was displayed in everyday life as well. If you kept a fit and strong physique, there was a larger attraction to you as a citizen because you were seen as a person who was able to do things better than those who were not fit. It was believed that your crops, iron, carpentry, hunting, and thinking would be better because you had more energy and strength to tend to those tasks. You were believed to have favor from the gods as a reward for your appreciation and upkeep of your body, the ultimate gift to mankind.

The Greek practices of fitness peaked during the Roman Empire. Massive fitness fields and gymnasiums were built for the public so that the people could stay in shape because the military draft was open to those between the ages of seventeen and sixty. And like today, the gym was also the central place to discuss business deals and community planning. Ultimately, Rome's demise was due to further concentration on their lavish lifestyle and failure to maintain a powerful society in strength and stability.

The Roman Empire fell to the barbarians from the north. A tribe, still adhering to the physical requirements of life, became more physically superior than the Roman army and overran them. It was during this dark age that fitness was revived because people had to resort to physical conditioning to tend to life, thus the respect and attraction for the physically fit was again a sign of a desire for success.

After the Dark Ages, great European leaders recognized the importance of being physically fit and made fitness a curriculum in every level of school as it is in schools today.

After the renaissance, physical education continued to expand throughout Europe. During the Napoleonic era, Friedrich Jahn earned the title of "Father of German Gymnastics" for his life's work. During that time period, Napoleon conquered much of Europe, including Germany. With its downfall to France, Germany was subsequently divided into two states. Jahn's desire for German nationalism and independence became a powerful force behind his development of gymnastic programs. He believed future susceptibility to foreign invasion could be prevented through the physical development of the German people. He also believed fitness was critical in Germany regaining its independence. It was because of this national threat that Germany started building and perfecting activities for youth fitness and competition, involving various abilities to determine who was good at each individual task such as running both short and long distances, jumping both high and long, balancing, climbing, and various acrobatic combinations.

In Sweden, Per Henrik Ling is credited for dividing gymnastics techniques into three groups: 1) military, 2) educational, and 3) medical. Ling used his influence, knowledge, and education as a medical professional to incorporate exercise into society for everyone. He spread the idea that each person should have an individual goal in fitness. During his push for a society more educated on fitness, he taught educators to obtain knowledge in human exercise, physical science, and physiology to improve the need for fitness.

In the 1700s, France, Germany, and Denmark recognized that the knowledge of fitness needed to become scholastic, thus the field of fitness instructors and physical educators were born. In Great Britain, the awareness of the benefits of fitness caught the eye of the king. So it was set forth that England would seek to unlock the science behind fitness. It was discovered that a certain level of fitness could cure laziness, complacency, and stress, and children who participated in regular exercise marked higher academic performances. It was also recognized that fitness was best dealt with on an individual performance level rather than group evaluation, allowing each person to progress at his or her individual pace.

During the colonization of North America, life was harsh. Regular physical activity resorted to variances of the past. Plowing the land, hunting, and other needed agriculture and civilization labor was the focus for a new nation. It was President Thomas Jefferson who studied and learned the secret of fitness. He was driven to turn a growing nation into a land of healthy, strong people. Jefferson condoned constant dwelling and encouraged climate adaptation for increased immune strength.

During the early stages of the nineteenth century, American education did not focus on fitness. The age of the industrial revolution changed the culture of America. Engineering and technology reduced the number of physical labor jobs. As cities grew and convenience improved lifestyle, the need for physical activity drastically reduced. Coinciding with these events was the rise of influenza, polio, and other death causing diseases, driving America to invent a cure that turned out to be penicillin, the last major drug to cure deadly infectious viruses and disease. After the cure of these diseases, the increased sedentary lifestyle of urban dwelling formed hypokinetic diseases never before experience in America. Those diseases are the major killers even today, which are the following:

- Cardiovascular disease
- Some forms of cancer
- Back problems
- Obesity

- Type 2 diabetes
- Osteoporosis
- Mental health
- High Blood pressure
- Heart disease

In the twentieth century, presidential leaders started making an example of fitness as an everyday part of life. But it was President Theodore Roosevelt who grasped the secret of fitness from a young age and supposedly cured himself of asthma with physical fitness. It was clear to him that fitness was part of the human DNA. Nothing was more foretelling to our country's leaders than the condition that we had reached. It was the first world war that illuminated the fact that our nation only had one in every three men in good enough physical condition to be drafted into the military.

This scenario had been the demise of great nations before the United States of America. Upon realizing this, the United States government quickly passed legislation to put physical education programs into public schools and fund nonprofit organizations such as the YMCA and the YWCA to promote adult health and fitness. But, like most great nations in history, the desire for fitness dissipated after the first world war and was replaced by celebrations, eating, drinking, and smoking.

Consequently, during this time of immense entertainment and partying, the depression hit, and the USA was in a free fall until the second world war. America had lost its power of fitness. It lost focus.

Eventually, a man named Jack LaLanne sparked the need for a healthier nation to restore the level of fitness that is required of a nation with great global responsibilities. Jack LaLanne understood the ancient secret of fitness and took it upon himself to plant the seed of fitness back into the minds of the USA.

> Probably millions of Americans got up this morning with a cup of coffee, a cigarette, and a doughnut. No wonder they are sick and fouled up.
> — Jack LaLanne

It was during the 1950s that the modern fitness movement took shape. Focus on testing for fitness readiness was put in place for young adults. Testing revealed that a staggering 60% of all American young adults were unfit compared to only 9% of European young adults. Increased council on physical fitness was added to the national government. National and local government gave financial incentives to open gyms and fitness centers.

It was at this time that the power of fitness was revolutionized, paving a way for America to undergo a transformation from unfit to fit.

But the secret to fitness had yet to be revealed during that growth until now. The time has come for all to be reminded that the greatness of any country is in its people, and the fitter the people, the greater the country will be. America has built the greatest infrastructure for individual and group fitness in the world.

With the secret to fitness just a choice away, any person in America can empower his or herself through fitness.

The USA holds the strongest presence in the modern Olympics. The Olympics were originally designed as a peaceful way to display each country's physical might and strength, but this is not the case in the USA anymore. The USA is no longer as fit as it should be. While it still has a vast number of Olympians, its body of people are still in grave physical condition should there ever be a need to serve the nation in a military draft. It is up to households and individuals to implement a satisfactory level of personal fitness for the self-preservation of freedom and democracy, a power that was built by the secrets of ancient fitness.

The focus on health and fitness became such an issue that in 2002, the Secretary of Health and Human services in the United States government created Executive Order 13545—President's Council on Fitness, Sports, and Nutrition—which is to increase fitness, economic work production and commerce, and individual financial success; build stronger community values; remain a top competing nation as a whole; and avoid societal and financial collapse. The creators of this executive order realized that the secret of a strong nation lies in the strength, capability, and physical capacity of its citizens.

With all of that said, you might understand how in every society, health and physical fitness is considered to be its most valuable asset for success. And in a free society, the responsibility to be fit and have success is in your own hands.

CHAPTER 12

Financial Fitness

If health is wealth then wealth is a part of your overall well-being, and by now, you should know that my philosophy of the fitness mind encompasses success in all aspects of your life, including your money matters. Financial fitness is a phrase I use to define one's financial well-being. Your financial well-being is not determined by how much money you earn or how much money you have; it is about how your money effects the quality of your life.

As a personal fitness trainer, my objective is to help people accomplish physical goals that will give them strength and stamina so that they can look good and improve their overall health and well-being. I will help them cut the fat and build muscle so that they can move through life easier, stronger, faster, and with more flexibility to enjoy the satisfaction of their hard work. This perspective is also parallel to your financial world.

If you're taking the first steps in becoming healthier, you should also treat your finances in the same fashion. Maybe you're fit physically and financially, or maybe you are successful in your area of finance and have everything well under control but poor in the fitness and health habits. Also, there are people who are fit but are careless with their money. In this chapter, you will see the similarities and how you can make positive changes in both simultaneously. If you're taking responsibility for your fitness, why not use the same principals and apply that same responsibility to your finances?

The gravity of finances might exist in the form of being in debt, being broke, or being without cash for immediate demands by creditors. The stress and pressure you feel is the gravity in your financial situation. This is the very gravity that can lead to a number of health problems. Headaches, anxiety, chest pains, restlessness, and sleep deprivation can all be attributed to financial difficulties or your financial gravity. Just as obesity is the number one cause of cardiovascular disease, financial stress is equally powerful in causing heart problems. If you are dealing with both financial and health issues then the gravity is doubled.

To remedy areas of gravity in your fitness and financial needs, you must focus more heavily on your habits. The new habits in fitness will help you develop better behavior with your finances, thus creating a more efficient lifestyle.

When you exercise you become more sensitive to what your body does. You become aware of its strengths and capabilities. Financial fitness is the same. When you practice financial fitness, you become aware of how strong your finances are and what they are capable of.

Just like the rewards of fitness should make you feel good, so should the money you earn. It should give you the feeling of strength and increase your motivation as you achieve both short-term and long-term financial success.

If you can recognize your weaknesses in your health, you should apply that same scrutiny to your finances. Take a closer look at your frivolous spending habits—the fat—and cut it. Just as you build muscle and harness strength at the gym, your savings can be that reserve energy for when you need it most. Being financially fit will give you the courage to do things you have not done.

Financial fitness requires consistency and perseverance just as in physical fitness. Building your financial muscle takes time and requires patience. Even if you strike it rich, you must learn to secure your financial muscle so that you don't lose it. As with food in our modern society, the availability of extending your finances has its conveniences as well. If you're not careful, you can become financially obese with credit and loans adding to your financial weight, and like fat in the human body, this debt can begin to cause problems to both your financial health and your biological health.

In the gym, I see people come in and try to use too much weight or exercise too much in the beginning and injure themselves. You can also overuse your finances and injure yourself. I have seen many people achieve great muscle mass, but when they go to the doctor, their cholesterol or blood pressure is high, or their stress test is alarming. The outside can look good, but the most important thing is that the inside is healthy.

You can have a big house and a luxurious car and acquire a lot of stuff, but if you are barely able to keep and maintain them, your financial health is poor. People making a decent salary can live the life of wealth, and millionaires can live the life of poverty, meaning they are worried about paying bills or losing their home. That physical pressure on the millionaire is the same pressure of someone barely making it. In fact, that particular millionaire has put his or herself in a position of barely making it, making his or herself financially unfit.

When you obtain a fitness mind and apply those same principles to your financial world, you will see the similarities of fitness with finances.

The good news is that you have the power to increase your financial strength. As in fitness, if you focus on the problems in your physique, you might get discouraged, but if you focus on the rewards of working out, you'll feel more optimistic to get started. If you have a hard workout followed by proper rest and nutrition, it will give you positive results. The same is true for your finances. Earning a good or even decent living followed by proper spending, savings habits, and financial nutrition, if you will, can yield positive results. On the other hand, earning a good living followed by over extending your earnings will give you negative results, and the debt you accrued makes you financially overweight. However, if you focus more on your financial goals and less on the debt, you'll be more likely to achieve success.

Nobody is going to rescue you from your unhealthy behavior, nobody is going to rescue you from your financial situation, but you. If you make an effort to develop habits in your fitness and finances, you will have positive and rewarding effects in your life. It's up to you to make that first move.

Whenever I start someone on their fitness journey, I start them on exercises that their body has done in the past, whether it was recently or quite some time ago. That is because the body responds to it faster than new exercises. Once the mind's reward system has been stimulated, we move on to different exercises. I call that the area of physical understanding.

>
>
> **The chains of habit are too light to be felt until they are too heavy to be broken.**
> **— Warren Buffet**

Finances work the same way. If you start with an area of financial understanding, something you know is rewarding, like saving a portion of your earnings for retirement, you will see progress with each deposit into that account.. If you start with something you don't understand, i.e. stock market, senseless gambling, or spending on trendy items or shady investments, your risk of loss on a return is high. Take your time to evaluate your circumstance or situation and find what works for you. Even if you have to start with a bedside piggy bank.

>
>
> **You will never get in shape with exercise alone, and you will never become financially fit by saving alone.**

Saving money is not hard. It's making the effort to do so that is tough because like in our quest for weight loss or physical changes to our body we want instant gratification. As you know, anything worth having is worth waiting for and working for. So you must evaluate your situation, educate yourself on how you can accomplish your financial goals and set your mind to make the effort.

Increase the power of your money making machine. In fitness, when you leave the gym your body's metabolism is still burning calories so you can lose weight. You can even double your efforts if you carry out a good nutritional plan and get good rest. Your body is still rewarding you by burning even more calories when you go to sleep. You can also reap rewards in your sleep from a portion of your earnings. In the financial world, this is called compounding. If you reinvest your investment dividends, you are doubling your rewards on your money. You must also superset your financial savings, or as I would say, you must super invest. In fitness, when you superset, your body must adapt and grow stronger to keep up. The effort that your body goes through to get stronger increases. And for every percentage of muscle mass you acquire, your strength grows exponentially. In financial investing, when you compound invest you multiply the increases of your investments. Just as supersets in fitness may require you to be more aggressive in movement, so does your money in compound investing. It becomes more aggressive and reaps larger rewards or results.

While I am no financial guru, I have managed to pick up a few tips from financial professionals, and I study some of America's most successful investors. But most of all, I've learned from personal experience how finances can directly affect your well-being and outlook on life.

I had worked for Paramount Pictures for over ten years as a personal trainer to celebrities and high powered executives. It was a dream job since I love what I do and got to see my work on the silver screen in terms of the stars' physiques. I got invited to exclusive parties and movie premieres, and I hobnobbed with the best in the business. And to top it off, it was a great time to be in the fitness business because everyone wanted to get in and stay in shape.

> America provides an environment that lets more people realize their potential than any other environment in the world.
> Warren Buffet

My income as a personal trainer in Hollywood couldn't have gotten any better, and it didn't. In fact, things changed quickly after there was a regime change at Paramount. I found myself no longer a manger of the studio gym and no longer a go-to trainer for directors and their stars. Although I still had gained a wealth of experience, my income took a hit. And since I had recently married, I began to flounder a bit, wondering how I was going to keep my finances from falling apart while maintaining my lifestyle. Things had to change. I had to reevaluate my business plan on how to rebuild my clientele and keep a steady income. Saving became nearly impossible, and I realized how much debt I had accumulated when my income was compromised.

At the same time, I was also recovering from making a classic mistake of investing in a bogus entity. Following rich people, I had become friends with people who were throwing their money at this entity that went belly up. They could walk away from the loss without a second thought, but for me, I think it would have been less painful to have been stabbed by a knife.

POWER OF THE FITNESS MIND

On top of that my wife, an entertainment writer, didn't get the green light on a show that seemed like a sure thing. So as newlyweds, we were zonked. In love and in the red.

Luckily, I had some very loyal clients who kept training with me even after the Paramount shift. I couldn't have been more grateful for them, but I needed to do more to stabilize my finances. So I did three key things: I accessed my situation on paper, focused on what I could do to make a better income, and invested in myself. I took my personal fitness level to the top as an example for prospects. I took any extra funds I had to advertise, I changed up my training wardrobe to look more valuable to the clients I did have, and I asked for referrals. Soon after, I began training on several lots and private gyms around town and gained some of the greatest, goal-oriented clients a trainer could ever have. My finances began to increase, and after a couple of years, my wife and I both began to work at full capacity. We were able to achieve goals that we had hoped for from the start. Little did I know that these were some of the seeds that would start me on my quest for the "Power of the Fitness Mind." I have sense grown as a result of those life exercises and am much stronger because of it.

So if I may, here are some do's and don'ts that you should put in your fitness mind to help you with your financial goals. It would also help to be mindful of these things during some of your workouts to create a bond with this behavior.

Do not bow to the pressure of status quo of frivolous spending, especially if you don't need it or can't afford it.

Avoid insanity. If you're not achieving your financial goals by doing what you're doing, try something else or add value to your current work and demand higher pay.

Lose the weight of debt. Put your credit cards on a diet and use cash. Be a responsible spender.

Achieve financial milestones and security. This can be becoming a homeowner, owning your auto outright, or establishing a retirement fund, education investment, insurance policy, et al. These milestones can be achieved in levels. In fitness, you must set short-term goals to achieve your long-term goals. You cannot lose fifty pounds before you lose forty pounds. Apply the same principles.

Strive to achieve financial independence. This is when you can work if you want to, but you don't have to.

Some people won't start getting in shape because they don't think it's obtainable for them, and the same is true with finances. I have talked countless people into believing that achieving financial success is possible. Once they believed it, they were able to achieve it! If you feel you can't achieve financial success on your own, seek professional finance counsel, but don't let your greatest failure be not taking action.

I believe that, through knowledge and discipline, financial peace is possible for all of us.
— Dave Ramsey

CHAPTER 13

Successful People And Their Fitness

Studies have shown that most famous and powerful people conduct their fitness needs early in the morning before they begin their work day. It is a way to start the body's engine and warm it up, to arrive at the office or workplace fully awake and not half asleep. They are energized and most likely in a good mood. This type of behavior is how people get ahead. The person who simply relies on coffee to wake up usually isn't fully awake when they arrive to work and isn't at productive speed until two hours later. That only leaves one to two hours before break or lunch. So in productivity, they are only using 60-70% of their work time efficiently. However, those who arrive after a workout are at a 100% productive speed and can do something extra for their own advancement in their job or life. The mere presence of an alert person energizes others to attention. This type of energy is the secret trait to leadership qualities and leading by example.

>
> The most important quality of a leader is that of being acknowledged as such. All leaders whose fitness is questioned are clearly lacking in force.
> — Andre Maurois

That doesn't mean that if you workout in the evening, you aren't or can't be successful. That was just a statistic. I actually have a highly successful client who's a business owner, and his only available time to workout is in the evenings. He's consistent three days a week and finds that time to work best for him. The pros of working out at night are that the body is already warm from the day's activities and has consumed the necessary calories for that day, so the energy is readily available for a good workout. Another pro for people who workout in the evening is that it provides a great stress relief both physically and mentally for a good night's rest, which is very important for weight loss. I've also found that once people have been consistent with their regime, they are happier to workout because they know the rewards of the relief they feel before they turn in for the night. Consistency and attitude count for every successful person, whether you choose to workout in the morning or evening or whenever you can. Just get it in and stick with it!

It is estimated that 76% of wealthy people exercise four days a week while only 23% of poor people do the same. For some examples and inspiration, below is a list of successful people in the world, their success story with health and fitness, and how it helped them to become who they are.

Oprah Winfrey has mentioned that she does a minimum of forty-five minutes of cardiovascular training followed by at least forty minutes of strength training with her personal trainer a minimum of five days a week most weeks.

Richard Branson, CEO of Virgin, was asked how he stayed productive, and he replied, "Workout!" Richard is a lifetime fitness mind. His physical activities include weight lifting, swimming, Bikram yoga, rock climbing, and running. Richard also incorporates a fitness lifestyle into his business model for success and encourages his employees to do the same. Richard also enjoys tennis and kitesurfing.

Mark Cuban is the owner of the Dallas Mavericks basketball team. To stay on top of his billion-dollar empire, he commits to at least an hour a day five days a week of fitness training, focusing on strength training, kickboxing, and aerobic classes for an all-round fitness lifestyle.

Bill Gates is a treadmill man. Every morning, Bill does about sixty to eighty minutes of vigorous treadmill work while taking in educational and world news subjects, killing two birds with one stone. It's kind of like having two windows open on your computer at the same time.

Hillary Clinton, former first lady, former Secretary of State, and former New York senator, has accomplished many things. To keep herself fit for success, she works out with her personal trainer at least three times a week at 6:00 am. On the weekends, she focuses on yoga with an instructor at home in New York.

Aaron Patzer, founder of Mint.com, lifts weights, runs, and climbs. He said, "You cannot work constant fourteen-hour days without a good workout at the beginning or break in your day."

Michael Corbat, CEO of Citigroup, uses the Spartacus Workout, a workout that includes, squats, push-ups, and dumbbell lifts with a fifteen-second rest in between sets.

Bipasha Basu, an American fashion model, said, "When I started out as a model, I took things for granted. Because I bagged work thanks to my looks, I didn't give my body any importance. I was a couch potato who'd eat anything. Then, in 2005, a tabloid ran a story calling me fat. I thought, 'I'm famous. How can I be fat?' It was a slap. I decided to get fit."

Stone Gossard, lead guitarist for the American rock band, Pearl Jam, said, "I think if you exercise, your state of mind is usually more at ease, ready for more mental challenges. Once I get the physical stuff out of the way it always seems like I have more calmness and better self-esteem."

Wilhelm von Humboldt, philosopher and founder of the University of Berlin, said, "True enjoyment comes from activity of the mind and exercise of the body; the two are ever united."

Thomas Jefferson, the third United States president, once claimed to have cured himself of asthma with exercise. He said, "Leave all the afternoon for exercise and recreation, which is as necessary as reading. I will rather say more necessary because health is worth more than learning."

These great people and others have relied on fitness to create and carry them through their amazing careers. With your fitness mind, you have the strength, focus, and stamina to reach these levels of success as well. It is never too late to start on a fitness journey that can help guide you to new, successful heights in life.

CHAPTER 14

Positivity Is Everything

One of the great things about my job as a personal trainer is that I get to learn from my clients as much as they learn from me, and from one of the Incredible 20, I learned to never underestimate the power of positivity.

I thought I was a pretty positive minded person until I trained a movie star from India. While he was seeking anonymity in America, I trained him for the duration of his stay. He experienced a sense of normalcy here because he is so popular in India that he couldn't go anywhere without mobs of people rushing to him. Although he appreciated the attention, he also enjoyed working out without having to look over his shoulders, which made his sessions more relaxed and open for dialogue.

This young man's perspective on positivity made me look like a rookie. He taught me how to adjust my view to see positivity in every single thing. Good or bad, small or large, every situation, including chance meetings with anyone who crossed my path, was an opportunity to see how I might enjoy, grow, learn, and find something to be grateful for, thus finding the positive gem.

It was no wonder he was successful at his craft. He was a person who possessed great self-satisfaction, saw beauty, and sought opportunity for positive outcomes from every angle.

What's most shocking is that he has amassed great financial wealth yet valued nothing material. He had conditioned his mind to see the good in all people and isn't afraid to communicate with anyone. He strives to maintain a perfect vision of good. My time with this client was priceless. My work with him was very enlightening.

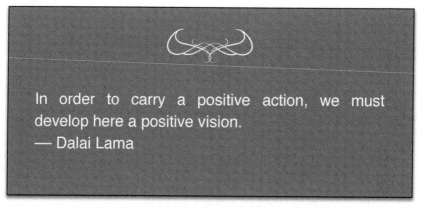

In order to carry a positive action, we must develop here a positive vision.
— Dalai Lama

In paying it forward, I encourage you to incorporate positivity as one of your new habits. In doing so, remove all negative words, actions, and bad habits that perpetuate a negative outcome and replace them with positive visions, thoughts, and actions. You must believe that change is possible and doable, and you must follow it up with a positive mental attitude and action. Your success in health and fitness deeply depend on it to create strong, new habits for positive results. For the purposes of your health and fitness needs, I want you to focus on two areas to interject positivity, your nutrition and your behavior.

NUTRITION

In your quest for better health, paying close attention to what you're eating is paramount. Countless times I've seen people ask the creator to bless the food they were about to receive but never stop to think of whether the stuff on their plate was in congruent with what they were asking.

When you say your prayers at mealtime, I want you to take a good look at the meal before you. If you believe that your meal will give you the power to have good health and strength, it should reflect that request of your creator. If it doesn't, then your prayers might give you something you didn't wish for. In other words, if your plate is full of fried, greasy foods, laden with salt and sugar, and without real nutrition, how on earth can you expect a positive blessing? You might as well pray, "Thank you for this meal that I am about to sicken my body with. May it raise my blood pressure, give me diabetes, clog my arteries, slow me down, and decrease my health." If you are not paying attention to your weight and your health, it would be silly to think the creator is going to give you the nutrition of grilled fish and leafy greens from fried foods and pound cake.

Now don't get me wrong, I grew up in the south where enjoying these types of comfort foods was a staple in everyday meals. As the obesity crisis grew, I learned that comfort foods were to be eaten on a rare basis and not every day. So please, keep your eyes open and focus on your plate and be positively sure the food you are about to receive is worth putting in your body. And if you need to increase your knowledge about the nutrition of the foods you love or what you need to incorporate in your daily meals, the Internet is an easy place to start. You can find healthier recipes for your favorite comfort foods, and you can also educate yourself on how to eat healthy at any income level and for any age.

There are certain positive foods that you can eat to help you create positive energy in and around you, and there are negative foods that you can eat that can create a negative energy in and around you. Negative foods also have various side effects that can lead to certain diseases, which impedes on your overall success in life. Particularly, the western diet was designed out of necessity from rapid population growth and not science, leading to the industrialization of cattle, pig, and chicken products.

This chapter is not about whether you eat those products are not, but rather the way you look and interpret the foods that you eat. With the fitness mind, food consumption should be directly connected to your quest for ultimate success. When you successfully obtain your dreams, you will be in a much better state of spirit when your body obtains its proper state of health.

As a personal trainer, I have seen countless times when people come to me after obtaining success, and they are looking for a chance to improve their health because of something that went wrong, something like high blood pressure, a mild heart attack, diabetes, stress, obesity, cancer, depression, chronic fatigue, and other things. All these things can be avoided with a fitness mind attitude and a positive perspective about nutrition.

Your body is a biological machine. Machines require precise forms of energy to function properly throughout their lifespan. Failure to provide exactly what they need consistently will lead to a breakdown, and that is what the human body does when you don't replenish its energy stores. I'm not saying there isn't any wiggle room for fun, but fun is not a reason for being blind to the fact that day by day, bad nutritional habits can lead to your body breaking down. And you can't say, "My grandmother ate chocolate cake and ice cream every day of her life and lived to be one hundred and twenty." The chances of you or anybody else being that lucky are few and far between in these days of modified foods. Besides, grandma was most likely more physically active than we are on any given day.

Your nutrition intake should be 75% plant base. Period. Plants are still in a life state when you eat them. Animals are not. The difference is eating life versus eating death. The body breaks down plant-based foods with no side effects if eaten in moderation. The whole plant source is the complete food product to consume and not the individual chemical components. The natural and human intellectual evolution of each edible plant contributes to the improved health of the human body.

> We struggle with eating healthy, obesity, and access to good nutrition for everyone. But we have a great opportunity to get on the right side of this battle by beginning to think differently about the way that we eat and the way that we approach food.
> — Marcus Samuelsson

The secret is in the assembly of properties during the growth cycle of the plant and the breakdown of those properties in the body that gives us that positive energy. Other man-made nutritional products might fill the brain's frontal cortex with feel good potions, but those products are also saturating your brain and keeping it from experiencing natural satisfaction from plant-based foods. The more you saturate your frontal lobe with sugars, the more you are leaving yourself open for depression and the need for more sugar. Once the gravity of that cycle starts, it takes large amounts of energy to break the cycle.

In your fitness mind, your nutrition is aligned with your day to day energy and the results that you accomplish each day, not too much and not too little.

When you see how important nutrition is to obtaining your dreams, you will start to seek those good food groups that the body was designed to consume. If you are committed to your quest for success in life, you will set your sights on more plant-based foods and a positive nutritional lifestyle.

BEHAVIOR

Increasing the fitness of your positive self, or getting your positive self into shape, takes effort. But just like exercise, diet is well worth the positive results of health, improving and strengthening your positivity with the way you behave. You can overcome a vast amount of negative views by focusing on changing your perspective, which will in turn change your behavior and vice versa. Change your behavior, and you will see life in a new perspective.

During exercise in a gym or group fitness, there is no room for negative behavior if you want positive results. Because of the atmosphere you're in, you should allow yourself to embrace and participate in the positive activities. People are constantly moving at a pace to improve themselves, and it should be contagious. If your perspective is positive, you will generate positive results. If you decide from the moment you step in the gym that you feel intimidated and fearful of the people and environment, you won't proceed to continue. You must keep your focus on a positive outcome, and you will behave accordingly.

When you leave the gym, you should feel good about your accomplishment, and that's the way you should feel when you leave places where you go to obtain any goal. Whether you're studying to be an artist, engineer, doctor, or any other profession, you should constantly practice behaviors of positive minded results. If you consistently put yourself in places like a library, a lab, an art studio, a class, or a seminar, you should feel driven to gain positive results or knowledge. Whatever profession, design, desire, or idea that you have or want to do, exercising to improve your physical health with your goals in mind will enhance and magnify the quality of your results.

On the other hand, feeling forced or coerced into a situation automatically sets off a bad attitude and bad behavior, resulting in negative results. In us and around us exists the nature of polar opposites, the natures of the positive and negative and action and reaction. If you view the negative as gravity, you should be able to find the positive force and use it to pull yourself through.

The key is to approach everything with an expectancy of a positive result or outcome. If you'll take this approach, you'll begin to see how this new behavior can positively change your life.

CHAPTER 15

Fitness Minded Results

We believe that our muscles have memory. We believe that when our muscles achieve physical results, they remember things even if it hasn't achieved those exact results in some time. But should you exercise to gain those results again, your time frame to achieve those results would come quicker, giving you the chance to exceed. It's as if your body learned how to add and subtract. Then, years later, it decides to brush up on its math quickly because it has coded your experiences from the past to reduce time spent doing the same thing. That is how powerful positive memories can be and how they can drastically enhance your life even years later.

A programmer's main skill set is to reduce our rich form of reality down to a much simpler model of reality so that computers can execute that model as code. Many programmers and scientists want to believe that their brains are logical machines, but biology has determined that our brains are predominantly run by best effort pattern matching from a history of experiences rather than logic, meaning practically 100% of the brain functions from intuition based reduction. So the simpler your thinking can be done, especially on irrelevant things, the more time you will have gaining success.

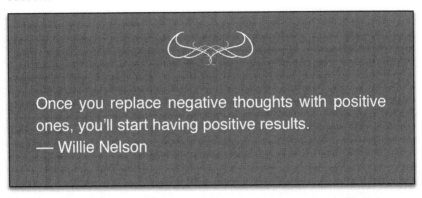

Once you replace negative thoughts with positive ones, you'll start having positive results.
— Willie Nelson

Your body operates according to the memories stored in your brain throughout its lifetime. Memories of physical activity and achievement give the body access to what it needs to improve, maintain, or return to the particular physical form. In other words, what the mind remembers the body can quickly return to faster than a body with no active memories of physical fitness or physical achievement. Consistently developing memories of physical achievement gives the mind memories to cross-reference for other achievements in different areas of your life, such as achievements in finances, relationships, social skills, and business.

If your mind remembers the amount of hormones it used to help you achieve a certain physical result, your mind also remembers using a certain amount of hormones to help you focus on accomplishing another task. The more memories you develop from accomplishing things, the more your memories can help you accomplish them again and again from a hormonal standpoint. So it is important to develop productive memories. When your brain's pleasure center achieves a result, it will benchmark your individual hormone levels to repeat that level of achievement, which is why you feel good after achieving goals. It is the brain's way of formulating a path to repeated successful events during the course of your life, just like a muscle memory makes it easier for you to achieve results again and again but much faster each time.

The only place where success comes before work is in the dictionary.
— Vince Lombardi

In fitness, one works toward results. In life, one works for results in the form of a return in value, whether it's by return in value for goods sold or a return in value for work well done. In fitness, results are the summation of all the hard work and dedication you've completed in fitness and nutrition. With other personal goals, success can work the same way.

The universe creates by using all the elements and all the forces together. That matter creates life. On earth, you must use all of your elements to create your own life. Whether it be a life of wealth, love, respect, personal achievements, or championships, you must use the law of the universe, which is to use every element and force. In the fitness mind, your elements are the following:

> ➢ mind
>
> ➢ body
>
> ➢ intuition

- inner energy
- perseverance
- determination
- knowledge
- natural born abilities
- relationships
- goodwill and fortune
- talents
- opportunities

All of these things are human elements and must be used while seeking to achieve success. In other words, the universe focuses all of its elements to create one thing: life. So you should focus all of your elements to create one thing: the life you want to live.

We are under the power and gravity of the universe. Its patterns move in a way that creates a beginning and an end. From supernova to galaxies being formed to life being born, the universe does not use time outside of its patterns or purpose. In the gym or during a workout, you should not lose track of time. You should flow with continuous effort until you have met your goals. In the fitness mind, you have developed a pattern of continuous success, so too in life you should follow or develop patterns of continuous success.

Micro habits are little things that we do day to day that keep us from goals. They consume time in the day that don't lead to personal progress. You must identify the micro habits that are consuming your time. If twenty-four hours in the day represented your body, how many empty minutes did you consume that will keep you from your goals? How many empty calories did you consume that will keep you from achieving your weight or fitness goal? That is the thought of the fitness mind. You must use the tools of behavior in life as you use the tools of your fitness routine. The effort to progress is the same.

I'll say this again because it is the foundation of your fitness mind: feelings and stress are part of our connection with gravity. Everything we are is because of gravity. We have evolved because of gravity. The earth exists because of gravity. So when we use gravity to help us, we succeed. It is here for us to improve.

When you exercise, your motion against gravity makes you stronger. In fitness, gravity and oxygen are the nourishing elements of your adaptation process. Therefore, in a fitness mind, pushing weight through gravity, whatever weighs heavy on your mind, heart, and body leads you to success.

Gravity pulls on us constantly, and each of us allows it to pull on us differently and to varying degrees. We chart our course in life based on gravity's pull on us. It is what draws us to each other. We are drawn to the gym because of gravity's pull on us physically. We are drawn to each other because of gravity's pull on our feelings.

Okay, so what? Why should we care about the effects of gravity? Because in your fitness mind, gravity is important for you to get stronger and better. The more you force weight in the gym, the stronger you get and more you succeed. Life is the same. Every situation in life is a weight that you have to lift. Every problem is weight that you have to lift. Every need is weight that you have to lift. Every goal is weight that we have to lift. Life is a workout. Every day is a training session, and every decision is a repetition in a set of an exercise in life.

Many people, when faced with tough times, think it is a test from someone or something greater, and in fitness, that something is the gravity in you. When you start pushing against it instead of letting it push against you, you get stronger and stronger until one day, you push through and leave that orbit of the gravity inside of you. You will soar through space and time on earth with very little effort, only making little adjustments here and there and experiencing your universe in happiness and satisfaction.

So when you feel gravity pushing on you, which is life itself making things tough, don't allow it to continue to push on you. Instead, go for life's workout. Push against it and keep pushing and getting stronger so that what's pushing on you isn't that heavy anymore. And then when something else gets heavier, push on it until you become strong enough to push your way out of its gravitational orbit. Every challenge in life has a field of gravity that you must push through.

In the realm of fitness, we consider the body first. From the day you are born, your body understands how to work before you are aware of it. So an individual's intelligence does not supersede one's physical life. Life is the body.

In our society, we damage the body as if it is indestructible, taking advantage of its fragile healing powers as if they have no end. The human body should be treated with respect, and even though it has tremendous strength, we must not forget how fragile life really is and how hard each body is working just to stay alive in this circle of gravity called earth. Our friendships toward one another should be a symbol of recognition of just how fragile life is.

In the circle of fitness, the common thread of understanding one another is that we are exercising to preserve our life, improve ourselves, admire our similarities, and respect our differences.

CHAPTER 16

Synchronized Fitness

In closing, this is a guide of how to turn your fitness behavior into personal success. Fitness has allowed you to acquire these qualities. Use them well.

Passion is the driving force that causes you to exercise for better health and success. You must find and use that force toward one thing that will bring you your dreams. It could be becoming an astronaut or creating your own product.

Do it for love, not money. In fitness, if you have the desire to get in shape, you will just start running or doing push-ups or sit-ups or jumping in front of the TV. In life, if you have a passion for something and you do it for the love of it, the money will come.

In fitness, when you are passionate about achieving results, you are willing to work hard at it even if you don't like the exercises. You do it because the results will be gratifying. In life, you must work hard at what you want and love the results it will bring, and having fun doing it will accelerate your results.

> Passion is what gets you through the hardest times that might otherwise make strong men weak or make you give up.
> — Neil DeGrasse Tyson

Get good at it. In fitness, when you get to the point where you are good at each exercise, your body responds with positive results like losing weight, getting stronger, looking better, and being healthy. In life, when you become good at something you are passionate about, you will receive positive results in whatever you are trying to achieve.

If you focus on repetitive exercises and good nutrition, you will achieve your fitness results. In the same way, if you focus on working hard at that one thing you're passionate about, you will achieve great results in life.

In fitness, you must push yourself if you want to get in shape. In life, you must also push yourself if you want results. Push through all your doubts, and if you can't push yourself, find someone who will push you, whether it's a brother, mother, or personal trainer.

In fitness, your labor rewards yourself with good shape. In life, serving others will reward you with wealth. Whether it's the next big thing or something already on the market, you must have something of value to offer others.

Most people who start on their fitness journey do so because they have an idea of how they want to look or how strong they want to be, but they aren't sure what the complete vision will look like until they reach that goal. In life, with your fitness mind, you must use your ideas that are generated from your passion and focus on that one thing to create a demand for your product or service to the world.

When you place yourself in the environment of fitness, like a gym or a dance class, you are able to take action. Your goals quicken because you are in a place to learn, listen, see, ask questions, solve problems, and make connections. You must put yourself in the environment of that one thing that you are passionate about and be willing to work hard and get good at it so that people will want it and demand it!

Fitness results do not come without persistence. Day after day, you must hit the gym and workout. That is how you achieve your fitness goals. That is also true in life. Once you know that one thing you are passionate about that can make you successful, you must persist. That means work hard through the criticism, rejection, and pressure until you hit gold.

In fitness, when you achieve that first short-term goal, you develop the power of expectation. Let your expectation be a spark each day.

ABOUT THE AUTHOR

Charlie Dannelly is the owner of FitnessWorks Productions. He graduated from Hampton University with a Physical Education degree. He is a personal trainer, an innovative fitness creator, and a patented fitness equipment inventor as well as an empowerment speaker, author, and life coach. Charlie draws from his wealth of experience as a captain in the United States Army, a manager of one of California's largest health and fitness chains, and a manager at the Paramount Pictures fitness center. He is best fit to take you through the world of fitness.

ACKNOWLEDGMENTS

It is with my complete gratitude that I thank everyone who has come into my life with love and understanding.

I want to recognize the following people for their unconditional love and influence on my life: My mother, Rose R. Dannelly, father, Charlie S. Dannelly Sr., and aunts, Precious Dannelly and Roberta Dannelly Durant. These are the loved ones who spoke to and shaped my conscience as a child and young adult.

Thank you to all of my clients who have come into my life for their health and fitness needs. Your pursuit to get fit has led me to many revelations that implored me to write this book. For you, I am truly grateful.

Thank you to all the gyms, centers, clubs, organizations, websites, blogs, magazines, sportswear companies, and stores for developing an ecosystem for people to flourish in fitness variation and style and for creating a world where people can develop a powerful fitness mind.